Bothy Nichts
and Days

Bothy Nichts and Days

Farm Bothy Life in Angus and the Mearns

DAVID G. ADAMS

JOHN DONALD PUBLISHERS

EDINBURGH

ISBN 0 85976 340 4

A catalogue record for this book
is available from the British Library.

Typeset by Pioneer Associates, Perthshire
Printed and bound in Great Britain by
J. W. Arrowsmith Ltd., Bristol

Contents

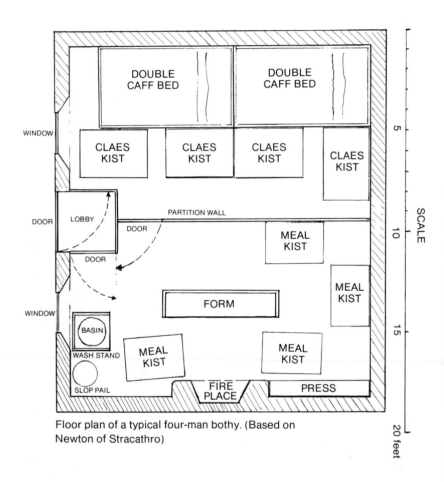

Floor plan of a typical four-man bothy. (Based on Newton of Stracathro)

Preface and Acknowledgements

THIS STUDY was originally inspired by listening casually to ex-ploughmen and other bothy chiels telling me of their life and times in the farm bothies of Angus and the Howe o' the Mearns. A great deal has been written about the *kitchie* or *chaumer* system which prevailed in the north-east, but no regional studies have been published about the self-catering bothy system which predominated in other parts of eastern Scotland and into Northumbria. The self-catering bothy seems to have originated on the larger farms in Strathmore (stretching through three counties) and the Carse of Gowrie, where it was in existence by the 1790s and possibly twenty years earlier. By the 1830s it had spread to other parts of eastern Scotland. It was becoming predominant in Angus and the southern Mearns by the 1840s and by the 1860s there was virtually no farm in the lowland zone of these counties, however small, which lacked a bothy. In the northern Mearns there was a mixture of the bothy system and what was known as the *meat in the hoose* system, like the kitchie system of Aberdeenshire and Banffshire.

It has often been said that the district in question was especially notorious for the state of its bothies but no comparative studies have been made to show if they were any better or worse than in other bothy areas. One general work on the social history of modern Scotland has claimed, on what basis one can only wonder, that the bothy system in this district was in decline after the First World War. Nothing could be farther from the truth. Bothies, improved or otherwise, prevailed right up to the 1950s and only from then did they slowly decline, becoming few and far between by the early 1960s. The very last ones were in use into the 1970s, although by then they were a relic of past ways. It was post-war mechanisation which brought the system to a gradual end as fewer men were needed on the land. The virtual disappearance of the horse from farms

vii

by the late 1940s did not immediately reduce manpower drastically since machinery and tractors were not as advanced as they became later, horse-drawn carts and machinery were simply adapted for tractors and many tasks were not mechanised until the mid-1950s.

This book is in three parts, the first traces the origins and early history of the system and is based on written sources and so it has been written in more or less standard English with a few Scottiscisms where necessary. The second part is based entirely upon the oral testament of a number of former bothy chiels, men who got their first fee from between 1921 and 1955, the majority between 1925 and 1935, and so the conditions described are mainly those typical between the twenties and the forties. It is written entirely in local dialect as it was told to me. This may have made it more difficult to read, not only for outsiders but also for local dialect speakers who are only used to reading and writing in standard English. However, I felt that the first-hand accounts from ex-bothy dwellers, which I have blended into a single narrative, would have much more truth and immediacy if retold using only their actual vocabulary, incorporating many turns of phrase, expressions and anecdotes, illustrating their dry bothy humour. To be continually using parentheses to insert Scots would be wholly artificial, and make it more difficult to read. Part three consists of appendices on the Horseman's Word, bothy ballads and local dialect.

The majority of my informants looked back on their bothy days with wry amusement, few with any bitterness. Many loved the freedom and camaraderie of bothy life, and if the pay was poor and some of the work sheer slavery, all who worked with Clydesdale horses enjoyed working with these canny and intelligent beasts, which were their constant companions for most of their waking hours, and took great pride in their ability to work with them. The attitudes of the local ploughmen described in 1813 must have formed from the 1770s and certainly lasted until the last pairs were sold in the 1960s.

I would like to thank all the lads who gave me information, lent photographs, and patiently answered my questions. It seems to have given as much pleasure to them as it did to me. Thanks are especially due to Andra Beattie for spending hours with me going over details and checking that I made no blunders. Unfortunately three of my informants, from when I first began to record such reminiscences about five years ago, have since passed away. I would also like to thank Hugh Cheape of the Royal Museum of Scotland, Queen Street, Edinburgh (another Angus man) for making available relevant files in his care. Thanks are also due to Charlie Allan, Little Ardo, Aberdeenshire, for the words, and permission to publish them, of *'It's lonely at nicht in the bothy.'*

Anyone interested further should visit the Angus Folk Museum at Glamis (National Trust) where there is an agricultural section with implements, a stable and a reconstructed bothy. Demonstrations of horse-ploughing, binders, reapers and steam threshing are given annually in mid-September at Drumsleed near Auchenblae.

1991   *David G. Adams*

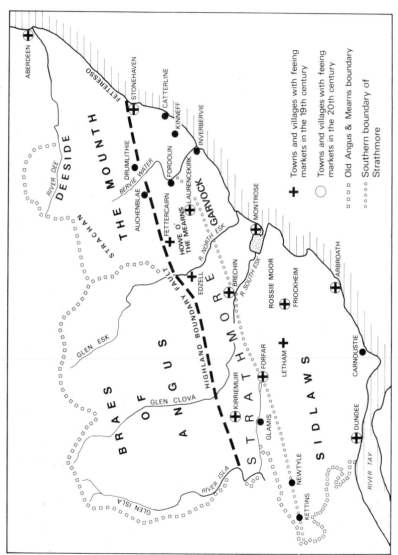

Map of Angus and the Mearns showing major geographical divisions, towns and villages

PART 1

The Origin and Spread of the Bothy System

The setting

ANGUS AND THE MEARNS have long been associated, as far back as Pictish times they comprised the single province of *Circinn*. As part of the later Kingdom of the Scots from around 850 A.D. they became a pair of provinces; Angus with the Mearns. Angus got its name from one of the three kindreds into which the Scots were divided, the *Cenel nOengusa* or kindred of Oengus (Angus) while the Mearns got its name from being ruled by a *maer* or royal steward. Angus was bounded on the south-west by Gowrie which derived its name from the *Cenel nGabrain* to which the royal house of the Scots belonged. There was never any natural boundary between Angus and Gowrie, although Angus traditionally extended from the Isla to the North Esk and the Mearns from there to the Dee, the exact boundaries have changed from time to time. From the 12th century the two provinces became the sheriffdoms or counties of Forfarshire and Kincardineshire although the old names continued to be used. The two counties were long associated but from 1974 Angus became part of Tayside Region and the Mearns part of Grampian Region although Angus and the southern Mearns at least, form more of a natural unit in many ways. The Mearns has often been considered a part of the north-east lowlands but it is only the northern part which geographically and culturally belongs to the north-east. Lowland Angus, and Mearns south-east of the Mounth or Highland Boundary Fault, is geologically, geographically and agriculturally an extension of the east central lowlands and not part of the north-east at all.

Angus has two major geographical divisions: highland and lowland, the former comprising no less than two-fifths of the total land area. The Mearns also has a highland zone comprising about a third of its area, and a northern lowland zone of non-sedimentary rocks, while just under a half forms a continuum with lowland Angus. The highland area of both counties is composed of igneous and metamorphic rocks. Much of it is between 1000 and 2000 or more feet above sea level. It receives 60 inches of annual rainfall although pierced by several river valleys or glens which are quite fertile in parts and have only 45 inches annual rainfall. The lowland zone can be divided into two (or three) parts: Strathmore, sometimes called the Howe of Angus, which extends northwards as the Howe o' the Mearns as far as Fordoun village; the Sidlaws, which extend as a plateau northwards to Rossie Moor and in the Mearns, Garvock Hill and the plateau north of the Bervie Water, all sloping south-eastwards into a narrow coastal plain, almost non-existent in the Mearns. The Strathmore area receives under 35 inches annual rainfall, 66% of it in the summer months or growing season. The coastal plateau and plain receive under 30 inches annual rainfall, some areas as little as 25 inches. Until recent times the mean January temperature was 37°F and the July mean 60°F. The region also has up to 1400 hours annual sunshine, one of the highest rates in Scotland. The climate can be described as cool temperate but the day to day weather can be extremely variable with snow showers occasionally as late as May and even early June in some years, while lack of cloud cover in Spring can mean warm dry days but night frosts. Along with the Laigh of Moray and the Lothian and Berwickshire plain it is one of the most fertile districts of Scotland, and one of the most productive agricultural regions of Europe.

The agricultural revolution

BEFORE THE GREAT AGRICULTURAL CHANGES which effectively became a 'revolution' from around 1770 in the area, farming was very different, with minor improvements a survival of the medieval system. Landlords usually leased out land on short leases, often to joint tenants who together supplied the animals needed to pull the heavy wooden 'old Scots plough' which required a team of eight oxen or six oxen and two horses to pull it. In the highland zone a lighter version of the plough was drawn by a team of six horses of the *garron* type. The tenants or *husbandmen* had sub-tenants or *cottars* who assisted them when required, and were paid in kind by being allotted land which was ploughed for them, with a cottage and kailyard, and were allowed to graze a cow on the common grazing. When the tenant moved, his cottars usually moved with him. The houses were rough clay biggins often with turf or heather thatch. Animals used the same door as humans, separated only by a wicker *hallan* or partition. The tenant's house was bigger and better but basically of the same type as that of the cottars, and they were all peasants together, eating the same simple food, and wearing similar homespun clothing. Single hired labourers were fed and housed with the tenants' family and worked and slept alongside their sons. The social and economic division between tenant and cottar was far less than that between the later capitalist farmer and landless labourer. They both had a much lower standard of living and were subject to periodic dearth or near famine, and on rare occasions actual famine.

The land was divided into the intensively dunged *infield*, nearest the houses and middens, and the occasionally cultivated *outfield* which was otherwise left fallow for years. Outside the turf dykes was the unimproved common grazing on which each family could keep an agreed number of animals. Few cattle could be fed through the winter. The cultivated land was divided into raised *rigs* on which the crops were planted with deep furrows between for drainage, which gave the land a corrugated appearance. Sometimes the lines of abandoned rigs can still be seen on hill slopes, especially after a fall of snow. The rigs were usually curved and sinuous with years of turning the long plough teams of oxen. Each tenant had a share of best and worst land so alternate rigs belonged to different tenants and were re-allocated annually. The main crop was oats, followed by *bear* (a type of barley), pease and beans gave nitrogen to the soil and variety to the peasant diet. In good years as early as the 1540s grain was exported to Norway via Montrose, while coastal shipping took grain from small havens in both counties to the Forth and Tyne to exchange for coal.

From around 1770 landowners began to lease land out for terms of 19 years in compact units to single farmers who hired labour. The system of six-monthly feeing for single men and annual feeing for married men was apparently started at this time. Such markets were mainly in the burghs but smaller places such as Edzell, Fettercairn and Letham are only known from stray references to have had feeing markets, and there may have been others at Bervie and Auchenblae etc. The old crooked rigs were straightened out. New crops and rotations were experimented with, alternating grass, grain and 'green crops'; potatoes and turnips. Sometimes the exact rotation was specified by the landowner in the terms of the lease. Lime had been applied to the land from the 17th century in some localities, to neutralise the acidity of the land, but became a regular practice from the 1770s.

In the old system only milk cows, breeding stock and plough oxen were kept over the winter, others had to be killed off and salted to preserve the meat. The introduction of turnips, which were regularly grown in the area from the 1760s, enabled farmers to feed large numbers of fatstock over winter, to be sold off when three years old. Most were kept in open courts, later covered over, and the dung and straw bedding which accumulated was used to fertilise the land. Turnips were first grown in a big way for feeding cattle at Milton of Mathers from 1754. The Swedish turnip or *rutabega*, which could be left in the ground over the winter, had been introduced into the Lothians earlier in the century, but was introduced directly into Angus at Mains of Dun in 1772 as the farmer there had a son in Gothenburg who sent seed over. (Montrose at that time had a great deal of trade with Gothenburg). Yellow turnips, a cross between Swedes and white turnips, grew bigger than the whites but couldn't withstand frost. Yams were grown in the 1790s and in 1813 to feed cattle, and it was said that they didn't taint milk like turnips did, but by the 1830s were apparently no longer grown. Potatoes were first grown in the district at Marykirk in 1726 by an old soldier returned from Ireland, but the method of growing them, or the seed, was not passed on, and they were only reintroduced from the 1760s. Although they were later in being accepted here than in some other parts of Scotland, by the 1770s both *neeps* and *tatties* were an accepted part of the local vocabulary, diet and agricultural scene. From the mid-19th century not only ware but seed tatties were becoming an important part of local agriculture and trade, to England and beyond. By the 1790s the old Scots plough and its ox teams had almost disappeared in the area. It had been replaced by Small's swing plough, much lighter and having a smooth iron mouldboard. It could be pulled by two horses, or on heavy ground by four. This was because the local horses or *garrons* were being interbred with Clydesdales but the results by the 1790s were not too good. A great many Clydesdales were bought in and gradually the more or less pure-bred Clydesdale was the norm by around 1840, although even then some horses were of lighter build due to mixed breeding. When horses first replaced oxen they only worked a single six hour yoke in winter from 8.30 a.m. to 2.30 p.m. and the men were employed in threshing in the early morning and late afternoon. This was still the case in 1813 but later was changed to two yokes of 4 and 4½ hours.

In the highland zone new breeds of sheep, the Cheviot and Blackface were introduced, and began to replace cattle as the main grazing animal. In the better parts of the glens farmers grew the same crops as elsewhere but seldom had a grain surplus, but hay and neeps fed the sheep in winter. By contrast sheep almost disappeared from the lowland zone for a time, especially in the coastal area, except for Barry Links, but by the 1830s hill sheep were being fattened in Strathmore, fed off neeps in the ground, enclosed by movable stake fences. Ayrshire cows were brought in for milk production, and selective breeding of the native black cattle to produce a better beef breed began. They had been rangy multi-purpose beasts, used for draught animals, meat and milk production. Hugh Watson of Keilor near Newtyle began to breed for 'beef to the knees' which was perfected later as the Aberdeen-Angus breed. He bought a black polled bull he called *Taranty Jock* and ten black polled heifers in 1810 at the Taranty Market near Brechin, and bred hornless stock. His lead was later followed by others but the breed attained its greatest fame by 1870 by the efforts of Willie McCombie of Tillyfour, Aberdeenshire. There was less emphasis on beef production in the district than in Aberdeenshire, and more on grain and seed tatties. All farming was mixed, rotating crops in four, five and six year cycles by around 1840, although a seven year rotation later became general, right up to the 1940s or later. Animals manured the ground which produced neeps and hay to feed them, nothing was wasted, there was no straw burning and no problem in what to do with 'slurry' as liquid manure is euphemistically called nowadays. Bone meal, lime and phosphates were applied to the land but few artificial fertilisers were used, weed and pest control were by manual or mechanical, not chemical means.

Even by the 1790s there was a threefold increase in the amount of grain produced in improved areas from thirty years previously. New strains of oats were introduced and barley replaced bear. Wheat had long been grown in the coastal area and on the south-facing slopes of the Sidlaws and Garvock up to 300 feet above sea level, but it began to be grown all over the lowland zone to a limited extent as part of the usual rotation. The barn mill, driven by four horses, replaced the flail on larger farms by 1800. By the 1840s it had been adapted for two horses and most farms over 60 acres had one, which included most in the lowland zone of the two counties. Many farms still have the circular buildings with conical roofs surviving, which once housed the horse-gang machinery. Others had water-driven threshing mills, a few had steam-driven mills, while a mere handful such as Bankhead beside Forfar, Bolshan and Dumbarrow in central Angus had windmills. Barnmen, who had once been employed to flail the grain, were made redundant. Some large farms had even had a barn greive to supervise a team of threshers. From about 1900 small paraffin engines were used to drive the mills for the weekly small threshings.

From the 1840s the scythe, used by men, was beginning to replace the *heuk* or sickle, used by women, which eventually did away with the large gangs of shearers who had come from Aberdeenshire before their own later hairst. The first practical reaping machine was invented by Patrick Bell, minister of Carmyllie, and was being used in his native parish of Auchterhouse in 1842 where Smith of Deanston's tile drainage system had been introduced. The reaper was only of use on level ground rather than on the usual rigs. Examples of Bell's machine were sent all over the world but it had limited success locally as rigs had still to be levelled out by tile drainage. This was only achieved from the late 1840s when Sir Robert Peel's government compensated farmers for the effects of the repeal of the Corn Law by offering low interest loans for drainage. By the time the flat fields familiar today were achieved Bell's machine was overtaken by the American MacCormack reaper, which built on the ideas of Bell, who refused to patent his machine. It was only from the 1870s that the horse-drawn reaper and later the much more complex reaper-binder made redundant the large gangs of seasonal labour needed at hairst time. The social changes brought about by the new agriculture even by 1790 were very significant, about half as many workers were needed on the land and about a quarter as many draught animals were needed. The surplus population was resettled in the towns and in the new villages which were founded at the time. They became weavers, carters, ditchers, dykers or day labourers, a source of extra labour on the land when required. Parishes with no substantial villages noted a drop in population in the early 19th century. This clearance happened at the same time as the notorious Highland clearances but here people were only moved a mile or two, and could easily find work and had gardens and a cow for subsistence, so there are no bitter folk-memories.

Steam ploughing with two engines hauling a plough by a cable between them was experimented with by George Greig of Hervieston, Kinneff, who set up the Kincardineshire Steam Ploughing Company Ltd. in 1866. It had six successful years but due to poor grain prices this particular company folded, although some steam ploughing was done in the area until the

7

1880s or later. Steam threshing however became common, operated by contractors who hauled and drove the machines and the caravan for the enginemen by traction engine, later by the diesel Field Marshall tractors, a common sight until combine-harvesters began to make them redundant from the mid-1950s. From the late 19th century American ploughs became popular, both imported and copied by local smiths, referred to as Yankee *ploos*. Even improvements in horse-drawn machinery gradually reduced the numbers of permanent and seasonal workers needed on farms by the late 19th century. There were once a few ten-pair farms in both counties in the 1890s, but eight pairs, excluding *staigs* in training, was the largest in living memory.

The emergence of the bothy

THERE IS NO MENTION OF THE BOTHY in the Statistical Accounts of 1790–94, which tell us a great deal about agricultural improvements but very little about the housing of farm workers. At Tealing in Angus single ploughmen were paid £10 to £11 annually with "*board*", which suggests that they got their *meat in the hoose* wherever they might have slept. In Fordoun and Dunnottar parishes in the Mearns unmarried ploughmen "*living in his master's family*" were paid £6 to £7 annually. At Kirkden in Angus it was said because of the "*sauciness*" of single servants some farmers preferred to employ married men whose family ties made them "*more dependant and humble*". In Kinnettles parish, Angus, there were eighteen farms but only 51 hired men, since it was said the farmer's family in most cases supplied labour, so some of the farms were still quite small. The farmers in Kinnettles who did have hired help only provided one or two houses with plots of land for married servants, and preferred to employ unmarried servants. But nowhere is the bothy actually mentioned or clearly implied.

Rogers however, in his survey of the agriculture of Angus of 1794 states that:

most of the farmers yet dress the victuals of their labouring servants along with their own, but this custom is growing into disuse. A practise now begins to prevail, of allowing them for victuals, 2 pecks of oat-meal a week or 6½ bolls a year. A Scotch pint of new milk, is allotted to each every day, and the necessary quantity of salt, or a shilling in its stead. When they return from their labour, in the house of the farmer, boiling water is ready for their use. They put as much meal into a wooden dish as they think they can eat, and having with the water, made it into a proper consistence, they diet in this manner thrice a day. Such servants as are more luxurious than the rest, sell part of their meal, and purchase what provisions as are more suited to their taste. This mode of diet gives less trouble to the farmer than the ancient one, is equally cheap, and is more approved by the generality of servants.

So in a long-winded way Rogers tells us they ate brose three times daily. Unfortunately he does not give the slightest hint of how the men were housed. Nor is it made crystal clear whether they were permitted to sit in the farm kitchen and slept in unheated accommodation around the farm, or if they had sleeping and living quarters with a fireplace. However, the provision of hot water from the farm kitchen may have been simply to save on the bothy fuel allowance in summer, since before the coming of railways in the late 1840s most bothy fires were of peat, or more often *hag*.

In the neighbouring area of the Carse of Gowrie however, the fully self-catering bothy certainly existed by 1794, although the word *bothy* was not used. The type of accommodation was described as a house adjacent to the *"offices"* (steading) where the men slept and prepared their own food. It would seem more than likely that the true bothy had also made its appearance on the largest farms in Angus and the Mearns by the 1790s, if not soon after 1770. The farmhouses or *"mansion houses"* as Rogers calls them, were becoming grander and no longer built as part of the range of farm buildings, which he said was *"unfavourable to elegance and health"*. Bothies were undoubtedly first provided on the very same big farms where such *"mansions"* were built. Most of the farmhouses existing in the district today are certainly mansions compared with the glorified cottages seen in Aberdeenshire. Few, if any, are as old as the 1790s, or have been so enlarged and remodelled from the mid-19th century, that earlier building is not visible. They would have been envied by a laird a generation earlier. The word *bothy* before the end of the 18th century usually meant a temporary shelter or sheiling-hut. The earliest actual use of the word to mean a permanent house for self-catering farm workers seems to be by Headrick and Robertson in their accounts of the agriculture of Angus and Mearns, both published in 1813. It was also used in the 1841 census to describe the quarters which housed twenty or more workers in rural textile mills.

Of the Mearns in 1813 it was said that single men were either *"boarded in the master's family"* or that they lived separately in a *bothy* where they ate and prepared their own food. Of Angus in 1813 it was said that single men *"frequently"* got their food in their master's house plus wages while others were housed in a *bothy* where they slept and made their own food. So the bothy system was well established but not yet predominant in the district at that time. The food allowances were as described by Rogers in 1794. In both counties the bothy lads got a Scotch pint (about three Imperial pints) of sweet unskimmed milk daily or the milk of one cow between three of them. They were also allotted either 6½ bolls of oatmeal annually (19¼ lbs. weekly) or two pecks (17½ lbs.) weekly and lived on brose or *cauld steer* and milk three times a day. In Angus they were also paid from £16 to £20 annually, costing the farmer about as much as a married servant, it was said. Married men got a house and garden, a cow kept and fed all year rather than a milk allowance, the same amounts of meal but also three bolls of tatties, or ground planted with them, and were paid from £12 to £15 annually, which was valued altogether at £33 annually. Their wives and children were paid for any fieldwork such as weeding, unlike the *bondager* system of south-east Scotland, where wives were expected to do fieldwork when required, as part of their husband's conditions of engagement. Single lassies lived in and were fed in the farmhouse, and around 1813 were paid £6 to £8 annually with 10/— shoe allowance for outdoor work in summer. Married men and those fed in the house had a slightly less monotonous diet than the bothy lads. Their breakfast was porridge or brose (with beer if milk was scarce). Dinner was of oatcakes, sometimes with butter, or with cheese, with milk to drink. Supper could be sowens, tatties, brose or porridge. Butcher meat and fish were eaten on rare occasions. It is doubtful, from later knowledge, if the latter were ever seen in the bothy.

It was said in 1813 that in Angus tea was never used in the bothies, but that married farmworkers used it occasionally, and farmers regularly. But it was said of the Mearns in 1813 that some bothy lads sold their excess meal in exchange for tea and sugar, which were in common use. There is unlikely to have been much actual difference between the two counties, but a minority of bothy lads may have drunk tea. The bothies, even in the late 19th century, never had kettles or teapots. No one could surely have consumed around 18 lbs of oatmeal in a week, the same amount allocated to a family. It must surely have been the practise from the time that the meal allowance was established to sell or exchange the surplus. Despite the ample if monotonous diet, farm workers were said to be a *"hale and vigourous set of men"*, although some occasionally suffered from *Scotch Fiddle* a rash said to have been caused by a diet entirely of oatmeal, causing overheating of the blood. It says a lot for meal and milk being the *basis* of a good diet that the men were mostly strong and healthy, but no one who had a choice in the matter would wish to live on such a diet three times daily, however wholesome and palatable. Oatmeal is an excellent source of protein, the richest of all grains, and also the only grain with soluble bran, while fresh untreated milk is a good source of vitamin C, although there was also a slight risk of tuberculosis.

Of the Mearns in 1813 it was said that a fifth of farm workers were single men, another fifth day labourers living in the villages, and the other three fifths married men housed in cottages on the farms. Of Angus in 1813 it was said that some of the farmers preferred married men, who were considered to be more *"steady"* and changed jobs less and were not always roaming around in search of *"sweethearts"*, but that others preferred single men, who complained less, and only employed a single married man as *"foreman"* (grieve). It was not stated what proportion of married and single men were generally employed in Angus. Day labourers in the villages were also hired on most farms in Angus for what can be called *orrawark*: ditching, manure spreading, haymaking and harvest work. When day labour became less common later in the 19th century, it must have become the custom to employ experienced horsemen as *orramen* on the same basis as ploughmen. Women also formed a pool of reserve labour, considered better than men at hand-weeding, or shearing with the *heuk*. The numbers of women *outworkers* as they were called, fell drastically after the 1861 census, as did the number of rural handloom weavers to call on at harvest time.

Around 1813 farmhouses were continuing to be rebuilt in more elaborate style and where the farmer was wealthier and his family did not work with their own hands he, or his wife, may not have welcomed farm workers at the same table. In a survey of farm workers' accommodation in Scotland made in 1814, Robert Hope of Fentonbarns, Midlothian, remarked that the bothy system was peculiar to east Perthshire, Angus and the Mearns. By the 1830s it had spread to many other areas of eastern Scotland, from the Lothians and Fife to Easter Ross and Caithness, but not to the north-east. It seems that farms with bothies were in a minority in the early days of the new farming, but as farms continued to grow in size by absorbing other farms and crofts, the system seems to have grown, until by the second half of the 19th century there was hardly a farm, large or small, in the lowland zone of Angus and the southern Mearns which hadn't got a bothy. In contrast with bigger farms in the 1840s it seems that, according to Ingles, on little places in Glenesk, where a single hired man or loun was employed, familiarity with the employer was such that they supped their porridge, brose and stovies from the same bowl! On the larger glen farms however, there were bothies housing both ploughmen and shepherds by the 1860s. In 1841 the farm of Baillies in Glenesk had eight male workers aged 11 to 55 housed in the stable loft, but this was about haymaking time and they may not have been permanently employed. However, in 1891 only two farmworkers and a shepherd seem to have been employed and all lived in cottages.

By the time of the New Statistical Accounts of 1833–42 the bothy system was very well established over most of Angus and the Mearns, apparently the predominant way of housing single men in most parishes in the lowland zone and the employment of single men was on the increase. Single men seem to have formed quite a large part of the workforce but perhaps not half as they became by the 1880s, as there were still many day labourers around in the 1840s but very few after the 1860s. Farms of 150 to 200 acres were common, employing three or four horsemen, mostly single men, as well as others. Farmhouses were of two storeys. Nothing was said of the standard of bothy building but it was said that cottar houses were *"neither attractive to the eye nor capable of being comfortable"* and that the constant moving of farm workers and the basic state of the houses did not encourage the cottars to *"adorn"* their dwellings. The cottages were about 12 feet by 30 feet inside and only divided internally by the occupants box-beds or other furniture. So it is safe to assume that the early bothies in Angus and the Mearns were similar to one Cobbett came across in Fife in 1830. Described as a shed with an earth floor, it had a single room 12 feet square with frame beds along one wall, a single door and window, and a coal fire, with coals lying in one corner. Coal may not have been so common in this district in all areas at that time, but heaps of peat or *hag* (brushwood) took their place in many bothies. Most may have had grey slate or tile roofs but probably no ceiling and undoubtedly an earth floor. Around 1840 a farm worker was prosecuted before the sheriff for leaving his job at Haughs of Kinnaird farm near Brechin because of inadequate housing. He had been expected to live in a *"hut"* 13 feet long, unplastered inside, having a mud floor, no window, a large gap beneath the door (which would have admitted rats and mice), and a hole in the roof. The sheriff admitted the inadequacy of this, but maintained that the man should have served until his six months were out. This would seem to have been a small bothy, and illustrates how bad accommodation could be. It would imply that plastered or lined walls and a window, apart from wind and watertight conditions, were expected as the norm. Food allowances were the same around 1840 as described earlier. In some parishes in the Mearns: Fordoun, Laurencekirk and St Cyrus, the bothy lads also got a tattie allowance. This was true in some parts of the Mearns in recent times, also general in Fife and Moray but never in Angus, where only the married men got tatties, despite the fact that it was a premier tattie-growing area. Some in Angus had as much as £20 annual money wages, but most in the area around 1840 got only £11 to £12.

Despite ample evidence that the bothy system was widespread, if not actually the predominant way of housing single men by the 1830s, it was said about the parish of Carmyllie in 1836 that married men were preferred there, although there were bothies in the parish. It was also stated that the bothy system, once so common in the lowland part of the county, by then was not prevalent, and that "*happily for the morals and manners of a numerous and important class of the community seems getting into disuse*". The conditions which prevailed in 'cauld Carmyllie' certainly don't seem to have been the same as in most other parishes. In Garvock in 1836 it was said that male servants had been banished from the "*Ha' board*" and were housed in bothies, a system, it was said, that had "*unfortunately found its way into this sequestered parish*". So it would seem bothies had spread from the larger farms in the Howe of Strathmore to the smaller ones on the plateau lands, and in Garvock, but apparently not in Carmyllie, had replaced *meat in the hoose* by that period. The economic advantages of the bothy system to the farmers are obvious, but they were, it was said, a disadvantage regarding the moral, intellectual and religious improvement of the farm worker, and, it was extravagantly claimed at Garvock, the bothies were "*hot beds of irreligion immorality and vice*". At St Vigeans in Angus in 1842 it was said "*it is however to be lamented that many of the farm servants having been bred from their boyish days in bothies and are but coarse and clownish in their manners*". It was also stated that the high rents farmers had to pay for farms, and the competition to rent them "*compelled the farmers to exact severe and rough toil in all kinds of weather, scarcely consistent with refinement of manners or much intellectual cultivation and the frequent change of abode was not favourable to their religeous improvement and demenour*".

At Laurencekirk in 1838 it was said that the farmers preferred unmarried men and that married men were forced to move to the villages, destroying the connection between master and servant. The difficulty of married men finding a house delayed marriage. At Fordoun in 1837 it was said that farmworkers put off marriage in order to save for the "*providing*" (the household goods and furniture) but that some couples had children before wedlock who were later legitimised on the parents' marriage, and that there had only been four cases of illegitimate birth in the parish in the previous year. This would signify that single men were preferred in the Howe o' the Mearns generally, since there was a distinct shortage of cottar houses. So it would seem the bothy was already in the ascendant in that area of large farms. In the Deeside area of the Mearns, agricultural development was later and there remained a great many crofts and small farms of 50 acres or less, giving any employees *meat in the hoose*, although there were a few bothies on some larger farms. In Fetteresso parish, on the coast north of Stonehaven, bothies seem to have predominated, but in the inland area north of Auchenblae there was a mixture of bothies and *meat in the hoose*.

The wealth created by the new agriculture went largely to those who created and controlled it, the landowners and farmers of course, but the farm workers living standard did rise. If the food of the bothy chiels in particular was excessively plain, they did not stint on clothes. "*Extravagance*" in the clothes of farmworkers was mentioned in the 1790s and in 1813 it was said that their best clothes on Sunday, when the men wore coats of English broadcloth, could scarcely be distinguished from that of their employers. Men and women on Sunday wore £8 worth of clothes, around a year's money wages. The old homespun and blue bonnets for men and tartan plaids for women was only to be seen on older folk. The young women wore printed calico dresses and fashionable shawls. At work, it was said in 1813, the men wore a grey felt or straw hat, a short drab coat and striped waistcoat with white or blue pantaloons or trousers and carried a watch. (Which could not have been cheap or mass-produced like the Ingersolls of more recent times.) In 1837 at Fordoun it was said ploughmen wore strong cotton or Irish linen shirts and a jacket and trousers of velvet (corduroy) or west of England cloth and a greatcoat of "*Scotch*" manufacture. The Fordoun ploughmen incidentally, had a friendly society with 200 members at that time.

The independence of mind of the single men, or irreverence and disrespect for those who employed them, and sought to control even their leisure hours and thoughts, was noted from the beginning of the agricultural revolution in the district, when their "*sauciness*" was noted, and the fact that married men were more controllable. The new landless rural proletariat may have been at the bottom of the rural social order (except for women) but the ploughmen had a good conceit of themselves, and took an inordinate pride, it seemed to commentators, in their skill as horsemen, especially with the plough, and in the appearance of *their* pair. This was natural since it was the only sphere in which they could demonstrate their skill and develop their native intelligence. The great skill of the Angus and Mearns ploughmen was noted in 1813, as was the fact that they were often sent to other areas, including Ireland, to teach the art of ploughing. The ploughmen, from the beginning of the new agricultural system, seldom worked without horses: ploughing, harrowing, carting etc. In 1813 it was said each man looked after his own pair of horses and had complete charge of feeding and grooming them and that the ploughmen "*display much vanity and emulation in having their horses in good order, and distinguished by the grandness of the trappings*". This was also a trait that lasted until the disappearance of the horse from local farms, their love of horses and ploughing which was their life. They could not have taken more pride and care in *their* pair if they had been their own. Of both counties it was said in 1813 the ploughman controlled their horses by verbal commands only, and that neither farmers nor sheriffs could force them to abandon this practice and use reins. When this changed is not recorded, but by the later 19th century the horsemen always made their own *rinds* from binder twine.

The bothy predominant

IT SEEMS THAT THE BOTHY, and the employment of single men was so prevalent by the 1850s that there was a potential future labour shortage. Mr. Cowie of Halkerton Mains near Laurence-kirk gave a talk to the Fettercairn Farmer's Club, published in 1852. In it he remarked that farmers were allowing cottar houses to fall down and were not replacing them. This, he stated, made it difficult to employ married men and so failed to create a base for the bringing up and training of good servants or to provide a reservoir of extra (female) labour at peak periods. He called for a return to the cottar house and the employment of married men and this was endorsed by the meeting. The various ministers who complained about the *"immorality"* and irreligion of the bothy chiels otherwise took no practical interest in their welfare. In 1852 however an unmarried ploughman aged 21 was hanged at Forfar for the murder of an infant he had been accused of being the father of. This inspired the Rev. Harry Stuart, minister of Oathlaw, and chaplain to the County Jail in Forfar, to give an address to the Forfarshire Agricultural Association urging the members to improve the housing and conditions of their workers. Stuart strongly advocated the building of more accommodation for married men, and rented accommodation for retired farm servants, who were forced to move into the towns to live in miserable garrets. But Stuart could see no alternative to the bothy for single men and only advocated minor improvements such as individual beds and bedrooms separate from the cooking apartment. He did not suggest that farmers, even on the bigger farms, should incur the expense of paying a woman to cook and clean the bothy, nor that farmers should feed their men in the farm kitchen. The self-catering bothy had become such an accepted and indispensible part of the farming system in the district that its abolition was unimaginable. The Earl of Mansfield had apparently built a 'model' bothy, of the type advocated by Stuart, at Scone. In his campaign for improvement Stuart apparently even contacted Queen Victoria and Prince Albert at Balmoral. Eventually the Association for Promoting Improvement in the Domestic Condition of Agricultural Labourers in Scotland was formed, in which several local landowners were prominent, while the president was the Earl of Panmure, one of the biggest landowners in Angus. The only outcome regarding the bothy was that Patrick Chalmers of Aldbar and Hugh Watson of Keilor apparently erected 'model' bothies, presumably of the type with separate bed cubicles, but these remained untypical. One of this type survives in the Mearns at Fernieflat, Kinneff.

The reminiscences of William J. Milne of his varied experience as a farm worker (and navvy) are a unique record from a farm worker's point of view for the period between 1832 and 1855. Milne was uncommonly serious-minded and articulate for his class, an avid reader and self-educated man, so his views may have been untypical. He often disguises the names of places he worked but gives the location. He also had what may have been a very unusual range of jobs, types of accommodation, and places he worked, not only Angus and the Mearns but in Formartine, Aberdeenshire, and County Durham. Milne started his working life as an 11 year old herd laddie, equipped with staff and plaid, on a one-pair place near Forfar Loch in 1832. The fact that animals had to be herded demonstrates that there was still unenclosed land. Milne was fed and housed in the farmhouse, the other employees were a maid-of-all-work and the farmer's two nephews. He later went to Letham feeing market at the age of 14 and took a fee as a sheep and cattle herd somewhere in central Angus. His hours were from 6.30 a.m. to 9 p.m. At first he slept in the farmhouse and was fed at a side table in the kitchen, sometimes with the son of the house, but was poorly fed. He was later made to sleep in a vacant stall in the stable when his room was let. His bed was warm enough but he had no light to read by. Even when he returned from herding soaked to the skin he was not allowed near the kitchen fire to dry his only set of clothes. His usual supper was potatoes in their skins with well-skimmed milk and small oatcakes. He then took a fee as a milk delivery boy, driving a horse, and was fed at the farmer's table with no stinting of food. He got his first fee to drive a pair of horses at the age of 16. After that he worked on a three-pair farm in Kinnettles parish, south of Forfar in 1845. There were five male employees who slept in a sort of bothy a *"considerable distance"* from the farmhouse. They were allowed to cook their milk and meal allowance in the farm kitchen, where they also spent their evenings, sometimes joined by the farmer and his family in song or dance. On one occasion the employees were admitted to the farmhouse parlour to be tested in their knowledge of the scriptures by the parish minister.

In the year 1846–47 Milne had his first experience of what he called a *"real bothy"*. The scarcity of hands in that period had pushed ploughmen's six-monthly wages from £5 to £9 plus the usual meal, milk, fuel etc. It seems that the dearth of married accommodation in the countryside had already caused a shortage of recruits for farmwork. The only utensils Milne said were in the bothy were an iron pot and ladle, a salt bucket and a wooden pail to carry water and to wash in. The meal allocation was kept in fixed girnals and when he left this bothy he only had his clothes kist, no meal kist as was usual in later times, if not then. In Fife and Moray the meal was kept in barrels but in this district by the later 19th century every man in the bothy had his own meal kist as well as a clothes kist. The only furniture Milne found in the bothy, besides the fixed wooden bed frames, was the usual wooden bench (later always called a *form*) in front of the fire, otherwise there was only the men's own kists to sit on. Milne said that he had never seen a table or a chair in a bothy. The only utensils to eat and drink from were a wooden brose caup and an occasional whisky glass. Milne remarked how it was a wonder that the downtrodden and despised bothy dwellers, with a razor and comb, a 6d mirror, shoe and clothes brushes could turn themselves out dressed and groomed as well, if not better, than their "masters". On the day the bothy bedclothes were due to be changed the farmhouse maid took clean sheets to the bothy when the men were absent at their work and was not allowed to make the beds for them.

One of Milne's major complaints was of the enforced prevention of contact between males and females on farms. Open association and honest courting was suppressed, which forced furtive meetings in the dark as if courtship were something to be ashamed of. He blamed this situation, and the lack of provision of housing for married farm workers, for the high illegitimacy rate. He didn't think much of the Rev. Harry Stuart's campaign for the reason given above, believing that more accommodation was not the only remedy. He condemned the greed of the farmers, the engrossment of small farms and crofts and the operation of farming solely as a money-making venture. He also condemned the social chasm which the creation of large capitalist farms had brought about between employer and employee. Milne left his first bothy over the ill-treatment of a horse. He became an under-gamekeeper on Aldbar estate near Brechin, paid 12/— weekly and was fed by the head gamekeeper for 1/— per week. His former employer, however, came for him with the police to force him back to his old job, but he only agreed to do so when his employer promised not to ill-use the horse any more. Later Milne expressed *as much sorrow at parting with a fine intelligent and well-trained pair of horses as ever I did in parting with neighbours of the human race*. He also marvelled at the *almost reasoning power* of these animals. Sentiments such as these would be shared by many an ex-horseman today.

In 1848 Milne engaged with a scything contractor in Angus. He describes how the squad cooked their own food billeted in a ruined castle, the women sleeping in the lower apartment, the men on the upper. This illustrates how itinerant workers always got the worst accommodation, not only then, but as late as the 1950s, Irish tattie squads in the district were often billeted in deserted bothies and half-ruined houses. Around 1850 Milne became a navvy on the Aberdeen railway and got involved in a riot in Drumlithie when the Scots and English ejected the Irish navvys from the village after they had consumed a barrel of stout intended for the former, as well as one allocated to them! After that he worked on a farm in Formartine, Aberdeenshire and commented on the strange dialect spoken there. He slept in an unheated ground floor *"chaumer"* next the stable and was fed an *"ample but vegetarian diet"* in the farmhouse kitchen, consisting of *"seven kinds of brose"*. There he had to water his horses at 4.45 a.m. and had to thresh until 7.30 before getting breakfast. He noted that some plough oxen were still used there in 1851. They had disappeared from Angus and the Mearns by around 1800. He noted that some of the Aberdeenshire farmers said prayers every night with their servants, who were banished from the kitchen after 9 p.m. But he said he had listened to a greater number of Scotland's fine old songs there than he had ever heard before.

In 1853 Milne went to work on a five-pair place beside Laurencekirk. It belonged to a Montrose solicitor who left it to the grieve to run. The bothy where the men cooked and ate had a tiled roof, through which the stars could be seen, and which let in the rain and snow. It also had a clay floor. But their sleeping quarters were in an unheated attic about 200 yards away. He said he had seen cattle housed better. Milne joined the Laurencekirk Y.M.C.A. and was the only member who was a ploughman. His workmates were vocal enough among themselves but could not be persuaded to join or speak in public. The grieve and the other men were amazed when their employer spoke kindly to Milne about his interest in debating the affairs of the day; the Crimean War etc., as it was so unusual for an employer to speak to any of them, except to give instructions to the grieve. Milne afterwards went to the Mains of Edzell where he had good pay and was well treated as to lodging and food. The census record shows that there were seven men in the bothy there in 1861. Milne finished his account of farm life by relating how he went to County Durham to work for a Scots farmer and apparently lived in a bothy there.

Only very slight improvements such as a stone floor, a ceiling and lined walls seem to have taken place by 1886 when John Duncan did a survey of Angus bothies. Most of the surviving bothy buildings today seem to have been built between the 1840s and the 1880s. They have stone floors and plastered ceilings and many have wooden pannelled walls, usually up to a height of about four feet, occasionally the whole walls and ceilings are so lined. Duncan described one dilapidated bothy near Kirriemuir which measured 16 by 24 feet with a grey slate roof and a stone floor, set *"between the caff hoose and a lumber shed"*. The door opened straight into the single room and there was a window either side, open for air. One window had a broken pane with an old sack stuck into the hole. On the back wall were three (double) beds to accommodate five men. They were unmade and clothes hung from a long line of hooks fixed to a strip of wood on the wall. A heap of hag for kindling lay on the opposite wall to the fire and coal lay in a corner. There was a small table, which was never used. A paraffin lamp hung above the fireplace, a clock sat on a shelf. Before paraffin became available from the 1850s whale oil or tallow cruisie lamps were presumably used, candles would have been too expensive. There was the usual *form* in front of the fire and kists took up much of the floor. Ashes choked the fireplace, but the men's only complaint or request was that they would have liked an inside porch or *"hallan"* to protect them from the west winds. Clean sheets and bowster cases were supplied monthly.

Duncan also describes how each man took his turn of week about on the *"pannie"* to redd up, fetch water and kindling and to make the porridge, or that at some places the loun made the porridge. He also mentions the clothes and meal kists, the flagon for milk, the *"timmer caup"* or *"brose bicker"* and (horn) spoon as the only utensils for eating. The only cooking utensil usually supplied was a large iron pot with a ladle. The porridge pot was set in the middle of the floor for the lads to help themselves, tea kettles, teapots or cups were seldom to be seen. The pot was used for all cooking and water boiling, the caup for all food, coffee and tea. Coffee was also mentioned in the 1860s as being a bothy beverage and in a book of poems of 1900, but seems to have been unheard of within living memory, although all the other features of bothy life described above would be instantly recognised by any former bothy chiel today, except that coal was usually kept in a shed or bunker. Duncan relates that from the 1860s grocers' and bakers' vans had travelled the countryside selling loaf-bread, sugar and tea etc. and that some of the usual meal allowance was exchanged for such supplies. Wheat bread however, was used to make steepies. There was no mention of jam, syrup, cheese or margarine to spread on bread, nor of the possession of a knife to cut and spread the loaf. According to Duncan the bothy lads were usually allowed to help themselves to tatties. The men were supposed to ask permission to leave the farm at night. The senior man in the bothy was expected to keep order and to stop the loun being ill-used. Duncan suggested no alternative to the bothy, and only advocated that more cottages for married men should be available.

The farmworkers' standard of living did rise slightly in the late 19th century. From around 1900 the bicycle gave them a new mobility, and after the 1914–18 war the Saturday half-holiday gradually became general. Food came to have a little more variety and the meal and milk allowances were halved, presumably compensated in money. Duncan states that the daily milk allowance was 6 gills (1½ pints), half that described earlier and the same as the *chopin* usual in recent times, so the meal allowance may also have been modified by the 1880s. The bothy system saw only minor improvements from its inception before 1790 to its demise from the 1950s. It became the dominant, and almost the only way of accommodating unmarried farm workers in the lowland zone of the two counties. While it originated on the larger farms, by the later 19th century it was found on almost all farms, and had become a regional cultural trait. The average size of farms south of the Mounth was 1½ times that in Deeside and Aberdeenshire, where even on eight-pair farms the men were fed in the farmhouse kitchen, although the farmer might have had a separate dining room. In contrast south of the Mounth even the smallest farms with hired hands eventually had a bothy. In 1881 for example the 56 acre farm of Middleton of Panbride near Carnoustie, employed only two men, who were housed in a bothy.

Whereas unmarried men in the district formed about half of

the farm workforce by the 1880s, and were virtually all the sons of farm workers, in the north-east unmarried men were the overwhelming majority but were mostly the sons of crofters or small farmers. In the north-east many of the farm workers aspired to a croft or a small farm, and resented any social pretensions on the part of the farmers, since they did not see themselves as an entirely separate social class. South of the Mounth the farm workers tended to accept it as a fact of life that farmers were as much a separate class as the landowners, and that there were three tiers in the rural social hierarchy. When some Buchan farmers took farms in the Howe o' the Mearns around 1900 and tried to introduce the *meat in the hoose* system they were familiar with, the farm workers resisted this, they were used to, and preferred the bothy and felt freer from the social control of the farmers. Another difference of attitude between the district and the north-east was that, in recent times at any rate, the few crofters were looked upon with scorn and pity by the farm workers, who preferred fixed hours and a guaranteed, if small income, to unlimited work, and an uncertain income on a croft, which might pay three times per acre for rent than was paid by the large farmers on the same estate.

PART 2

Bothy Life
Within Living Memory

Bothy chiels and ither fowk
aboot the place

The first pair upon the place
A swishin black and grey
The second a chesnut and a broon
The third a pair o stately horse
As ye'll see this coonty roond
And the fourth a pair o lazy bruits
That canna ging their roond

Sy Watt's the foreman, he's a strappin chiel
His horse and his harness are aye lookin weel
[1] Torry he's the second man
And up and doon the lea rig
He maks them ging their roonds

[2] Munday he's the staigger
It's him that yokes the staigs
And fan he gets them in the yoke
My God they'll lift their legs

1 Issac Torry
2 Geordie Munday

25

3 Taylor and Henry it's them
   That pu's the neeps
   And fan they're storin them
   They're strippet tae the breeks

   Polly she's the maid
   She's a canty buddy
   Fae Cairndrum the chappie comes
   That gets tae find her fuddy

Reidhall 1921

3 Bob Taylor gaffer, Eck Henry loun

FERMS WERE BIGGER in Angus and the Mearns than in the north but no as big as the biggest in Fife or the Lothians far ye got some twelve-pair places and as mony as sixteen in the bothy. The biggest place in the district wis Mains o Aigle wi 850 acre, aboot 500 acre o it arable, the rest hill grazin rinnin up ower Aigle Hill. Bowshin had 650 acre, a square mile, Mains o Auchmithie and Mains o Glamis were aboot the same, wi eicht pair and an orrabaist, and eicht lads in the bothy. In the Mearns there was Balmakewan, Hatton and the Bent a' wi five or six hunder acre and seven or eicht pair. The sma'est places were aboot 100 tae 150 acre wi twa or een-and-a-half pair. A pair o horse cud work 60 tae 90 acre, or aboot 80 acre. An average kind o place wid hae aboot 250 tae 350 acre so wid hae three tae five pair. Maist horsemen were in the bothy so ye micht hae three horsemen, an orraman and a loun in an average kind o bothy. The foreman micht be merried and in a cottar hoose as weel's the gaffer and maybe ae cattler. At Cookston o Eassie there were seven in the bothy: five horsemen and twa orramen; at Dunkenny seven lads tae but fower horsemen, an orraman and twa cattlers; Mains o Glamis had a bothy for eicht lads, at ae time fower horsemen, two orra lads, a cattler and a loun; Mid Ingleston had five pair but only three horsemen in the bothy as there were hooses for twa merried ploomen. Some places had a shepherd but nae offen in the bothy unless there wis a second

26

shepherd. Mains o Aigle had the maist men o ony in the district, sixteen a' thegither aroond the 1920s. There were twa shepherds there, the heid shepherd was oot on the hill maist o the time lookin eftir the yowes ootside, wis married and had a hoose. The second shepherd fed the hoggies, the year-auld lammies. He wis ca'd the feedin shepherd. Maist smiddies served a haill area or estate and smiths rented the smiddy and were there ain gaffer but a few places like Mains o Aigle had there ain smiddy and full-time smith. There were six horsemen, een merried and five mair and a loun in the bothy. There wis a heid orraman and a second and a heid cattler and a second and a gaffer of coorse, a' in cottar hooses. The fermer then, Dave Arnot bein bigsy kind, and ha'en anither place forby, had a strapper, an auld mannie, Sandy Middleton tae drive him aboot and look eftir the sholt. He did odd jobs aboot the place and fed the hens. He bade in a separate bothy ahent the fermhoose which had twa separate beds wi a fancy frame aroond them. A few gentry kind o fermers had strappers afore cars did awa wi horse gigs.

Maist ferms had a grieve, as the fermer wid ca him, but the lads aye ca'd him the *gaffer*. He wis responsible for the daily runnin o the ferm and the men had little or nae dealins wi the fermer, ye were offen mair faird o the gaffer than ye were o the fermer himsel. The gaffer gied the horsemen, orramen and loun their daily orders, whether they were tae ploo, cairt, thrash or fitever. He wis aye an experienced horseman. He had started like abody else as a loun himsel in the bothy and worked himsel up tae foreman afore gettin a gaffer's job. They were near aye merried, it was gey uncommon tae hae a gaffer in the bothy, Jock Skene at Ballochy and then Cotton o Menmuir wis an exception. They were offen very hard men and affa buggers tae work themsel, and aye made shuir ye didna hae a meenit's brak if they cud help it. They hadna haen muckle schuilin but they cud work oot tae the second foo lang it wid tak ye tae ploo a corner o a park and wid say *"aye weel ye'll hae time tae ca a load o neeps afore ye louse"*. The best o them were weel respectit for there ability yae run a place, but they werna aye liket! Fan they got alder some took on a sma placie o their ain. Some places, maistly wi only twa pair, but some wi three, had a *foreman-and* instead o a gaffer. He gied the orders but worked the first pair himsel.

Shepherds were their ain gaffers and left tae get on wi their sheep. Far the fermer was a bit o a horse dealer tae, he wid hae a *staigger* tae train the young horse or *staigs*. He wis aye a highly skilled and experienced horseman. He micht hae been first or second and had a special knack wi horse. He wis his ain gaffer tae, answerable only tae the fermer. On ony ferm half the lads were horsemen. If there were three horsemen there were as mony daen orrawark, the gaffer the orraman and the loun, on a big place twa orramen and whiles a big loun and a little loun. Horsemen held themsel abuin abody, even if the shepherd or heid orraman got peyed as muckle or mair than the foreman. Horsemen worked wi horse maist o the time, plooin, harra'in, or cairtin but preferred plooin tae ony ither job as it wis the maist skilled job wi horse. Whiles of coorse they had tae dae orrawark like spreadin dung, singlin neeps, threshin or fitever. There was a very strict order at work and in the bothy. The first horseman, or *foreman* as he wis ca'd, had the best pair o horse and he led first oot o the stable in the mornin and wis first back at lousin time and led in the field. In the bothy tae, the foreman, second and so on had choice o far they sat and slept. Ye didna dare challenge this, it was een o the few perks they had, a place o honor, as there wasna an affa lot o difference in pey. There was naething orra aboot the orraman, he got his title fae daen *orrawark* a' the time but he was an experienced horseman tae. Orrawark included onything nae needin horse like pu'in neeps, or spreadin muck but an orraman cud tak the orrabaist or a pair tae fill in for onybody. He wis content tae gie up workin wi horse and cud rise later and feenish earlier than the horseman, no haen horse tae look eftir. On a big place the heid orraman, wi the gaffer, wis in chairge o biggin stacks and makin tattie pits. If a field o neeps wis frostit that wis an *Act o God* but if the corn got weet in the stack or the tatties wis frostit in the pit God help the orraman! Cattlers were left tae get on wi their wark in the byre and coort a' winter. In the summer, eftir he had looked roond the cattle and didna hae fences tae sort, the cattler reported tae the gaffer tae dae orrawark, or whiles looked eftir the fermhoose gairden. Some cattlers were in the bothy but dairy cattlers were near aye merried wi a wife tae help them wi the kye. Horsemen jist cudna understand onybody that didna, or cudna, work wi horse, and said that cattlers were a' "*wrang i' the feet or wrang i' the heid*".

Afore the war ye left schuil at fourteen. If yere father worked on a ferm ye gaed tae a country schuil far every loun's ambition was tae work a pair o horse. Ye aiven yokit yere pals wi a bit binder twine as yere pair and played at bein a plooman. If ye were lucky ye micht hae gotten a wee shottie at plooin fae some horseman afore ye left schuil. Yere first fee fan ye were 14 micht be on the same ferm yere father worked on, so ye cud bide at hame. Or maybe yere first fee wis at the next ferm or less than a mile awa so ye micht get yere denner fae the fermer and gaed hame at nicht. But maist louns left schuil tae ging and bide in a bothy maybe five or ten mile fae hame. Some took tae the bothy like a djeuk tae watter but ithers grat themsel tae sleep for a week. Ye started aff daen orra jobs alang wi the gaffer, so ye pu'ed neeps, hashed neeps, fed sheep or cattle, maybe fed hens and collect eggs for the fermer's wife, or ye cud be spreadin dung or makin strae raips. Fan ye were a bittie alder ye micht get tae tak the orrabaist tae work the *bagwallopers* or tattie harra's, or ca a load o neeps intae toon. Ye felt like a young lad wid nooadays wi a car, awa yersel wi a horse and cairt at the age o fifteen! Be the time ye were sixteen or seventeen, seldom younger, ye micht get yere first pair. Then at last ye felt ye were a *man* but until ye were aboot twenty ye didna hae yere real adult strength and ye were hardly fit tae cairry bags o corn on yere back weyin twa hunderwecht or mair. If ye cudna get a pair ye micht hae gotten on for cattler, or second shepherd on a hill place.

There wis generally only ae maid in the fermhoose, occasionally twa, tae dae hoose and kitchen work and whiles milk coos. The maid wis under the chairge o the fermer's wife and offen wisna allowed tae enter the bothy door tae cheenge beddin and redd up fan the lads were there. Ye collected yere milk fae her in the mornin, that wis aboot the only chance ye had o speakin till her, but ye aye held in wi the maidie if ye cud, and ye micht get eggs or a bittie butter in yere milk can. The maid had a lang day, workin fae mornin tae nicht. She had a wee roomie in the fermhoose, offen next the kitchen, and got her meat in the hoose.

The bothy

THE SIZE O THE BOTHY and the number o lads in it depended of coorse on the size o the ferm. A few sma placies had a bothy for jist twa lads but maist had twa caff beds and space for fower lads aiven if there wis only twa or three lads bidin in it. Fower or five lads in a bothy wis aboot the average. Bothies were whiles bigget on the end o the steadin or on the end o a row o cottar hooses, but maistly they sat on their ain near the steadin, but offen oot o sicht o the fermhoose. Maist were built on ae level and looked like half a cottar hoose, wi a single lum on ae gable. Some had a door at ae side and only ae winda, ithers had a door atween twa windas. Some had a back winda tae but some had only ae winda tae licht the place. There were nae curtains on the windaes, if there was a broken pane it micht be lang aneuch afore it wis replaced, so ye wid jist cover it wi onything ye cud lay yere hands on. At Castleton o Eassie the tap half o the bothy door was missin for a term or langer aroond 1928 and there wis jist a bit sackin tae keep the warst o the draucht oot. The fermers didna believe in peyin for only fal-de-rals, jist the very basic accommodation.

On a big place wi six tae eicht pair, the bothy whiles had the beds upstair. Mains o Glamis had fower caff beds tae sleep eicht lads upstair, a brander abuin the fireplace lat the heat upstair. Dunkenny's bothy eence had seven lads in it, three sleepin doonstair and fower up. The upstair had twa rooms tae, een wi a fireplace in the dividin wa. Fernieflat had separate cubicles and beds for five lads, twa doon and three upstair. Balwyllo wis anither big bothy wi beds upstair. Maist bothies had twa rooms, whiles wi a wee lobby inside the door tae stop drauchts, the fireplace in ae room and twa or three caff beds in the ither. The flair wis aye steen. A lot of bothies had the wa's lined wi wid tae aboot fower feet aff the flair, some a' the wye up and the ceilin tae. The fireplace wis aye on a gable wa. There wis never ony reenge like ye got in a ferm hoose, jist an open grate. The coals were held in wi iren fire bars wi space aboot a fit or mair aneth tae lat the aise fa, the *aise-hole*, there were flat steen or iren cheeks at aither side, and a muckle swey tae hing the pot, kettle or fryin pan fae. The pot wis a muckle roond-bellied three-leggit thing like a witch's cauldron. It and a big black iren kettle cam wi the bothy. In the auld days some places had nae kettle or teapot so the lads had nae tea in the mornin as the pot wis fu o porridge. Far ye had a teapot it was the broon enamel kind, at Mains o Glamis it held a gallon! Fryin pans werna supplied but somebody aye had een. They were o the type wi a hoop hanle for hingin fae the swey.

The fireplace aye had a mantlepiece ower it wi a clock and a puckle odds and ends, bicycle clips, collar studs, pocket knives and so on sittin on it. The bothy wis lit be a single paraffin lamp that had a roond reflector that ye polished tae get the maist licht, but it gied a fell puir licht and didna encourage onybody tae try and read very muckle. There were twa enamel buckets for clean watter and slops. There was nae watter in the bothy, it had tae be cairried in, but of coorse cottar hooses had nae inside watter aither. There wis an enamel basin tae wash in. It stuid on a widden wash stand or a metal tripod. At Mains o Benshie it stood on an anvil instead, and ye were nae man ava unless ye cud lift it, so abody there had chappit taes! Ye didna hae muckle time tae wash and shave in the mornin so ye maistly had a guid wash and shave at nicht. There was nae ither furniter in the livin space o the bothy except a muckle widden form wi airms and a back that sat in front o the fire, sometimes happit wi auld jaickets tae keep the draucht fae the door aff yere back. Some bothies had the form bolted tae the flair near tae the fireplace so as tae stop ye biggin the fire up ower muckle. But ye maistly sat on yere mealer.

Abody in the bothy had twa kists, a mealer and a claeser. Yere meal kist wis aboot three fit lang, it had a section at ae end, aboot a quarter or a third o the space far ye kept yere bowel, spuin, knife, breid, tea and athing else. Yere claes kist wis aboot half as big again and it had a wee shelf wi a hinged lid far ye kept collars and ties. Aneth it wis a wee drawer ye cud lock far ye kept yere money and yere guid watch, if ye had een. It was considered bad form tae lock yere mealer and if the ither lads kent they micht coup it upside doon and athing inside, meal and seerup a' mixed up thegither. The senior horseman in the bothy got tae pit his mealer at ae side nearest the fire, the next at the ither side and the rest o ye far ye cud. Maist o the flair wis taen up wi kists. Ye sat on yere mealer fan ye were eatin. Bikes were kept in a shed or in the lobby if there was een, but whiles against the inside wa o the bothy. There wis a coal press hole and whiles a big press wi shelves. On ae side wa there wis offen a lang strap o wid wi a line o hooks for hingin claes fae.

Maist bothies had the bed space partitioned aff and it micht hae a widden flair, but ye were cosier bein open tae the fire. If ye were cauld in yere bed ye jist bigget up the fire at nicht or ye pit a het brick wrapped in a cloot in yere bed. The beds were jist roch widden frames filled wi a caff mattress. This wis made o blue and white strippet tickin filled wi oat caff fae the summer thresh eence or twice a year. Barley caff wis nae yaise and wheat caff wis ower stoorie and mice liked it a' the better. Fan the mattress wis new filled it wis aboot a fit or mair thick, but as ye slept on it, it wore doon intae yere shape. There wis a bowster for yere heid, filled wi caff tae. There were roch blankets, sheets and a bowster cover supplied. Whiles there micht be a cover made o knitted woolen squares, ony vacant bed had claes thrown on it. Ye slept twa tae a bed in order o seniority, so the foreman and the second shared a bed, the third wi the fourth, and the orraman wi the loun. Jist like athing else on the ferm and in the bothy a very strict order o seniority wis kept, the horseman had seniority then the orramen, the cattlers and the loun. Ye never had ony lavvy or dry oaffie for the bothy, ye jist peed some wye oot o sicht and shat in the coort and dichted yersel wi a wisp o hey or strae. Ye wid sae, *"I'm awa tae pey the laird"*. Aiven eftir the war, fan some bothies like Arrat's had a wattery, the lads preferred tae ging tae the coort, it saved haen tae clean the lavvy. If ye gaed awa tae the coort wi'oot yere bonnet on, some lad wid throw steens or tatties at the stots tae gar them rin roond the coort and disturb yere peace, so ye jist didna ging tae the coort wi'oot pitten yere bonnet on!

The fermer supplied coal and wid for the fire, paraffin for the bothy lamp, saut, soap, bedclaes and toowels. The toowels were that roch they near took the skin aff ye. Ye got a ton o coal a month, there wis never ony shortage and some bothy fires were never oot for a sixmonth aiven in summer. The stories aboot bothy lads burnin doon a tree trunk in the fire afore they cud shut the bothy door are jist a lauch, ye aye had plenty coal. There were whiles affa rows wi the fermer ower the heid o coal: "*Tae hell, that's only duin ye a month!*" he micht say. Only auld wid wis gien tae the bothy lads for kindlin, or ye hacked up ony auld wid lyin aboot the place; palin posts, stack bosses, or branches affen trees. Abody in the bothy took week aboot on the *pan* or *pannie*. That meant panwid or firewid but if it wis yere week on the pannie ye hackit sticks, filled the watter bucket, bigget the fire, made the porridge fae your meal and it wis yere week tae get the Sunday sassages and tae redd up the bothy and tae bide ahent at the weekend tae see tae the horse. At some places een o the merried wifies wis peyed be the fermer tae redd up the bothy, mak the beds and fill the paraffin lamp. She got a' the orrals; stale breid and porridge left ower for her pig. The bothy flair was scrubbed only eence a year. Ye were whiles bathered wi rats and mice, they got in through the coal hole or aneth the door. The senior lad in the bothy wis supposed tae set the tone and keep order, so the bothy wis kept as roch or as tidy as he liked it tae be.

Thats hoo maist bothies were afore the war and for a while eftir. Afore the war there were een or twa ferms that had diesel-powered electricity generators, Fithie had een that supplied licht tae the fermhoose and the steadin, but no the bothy, but at Balquarn and Shandford the bothies had electric licht. Dunkenny got a sma generator tae licht the bothy durin the war. Mains o Fettercairn had a watter-powered generator fae the muckle dam there, but again no for the bothy, only the big hoose and the steadin. There were only a few hostels on ferms belangin tae very forward-lookin fermers. Sir Thomas Wotherspoon had big tattie dressin squads in hostels at Balkeerie and Cookston o Eassie wi aboot sixteen lads in each. A lot o them were fae Harris, affa fine lads, Gaelic speakers. They had a wifie tae mak meat for them, a dining room, living room, a bathroom wi a het watter boiler and bedrooms upstairs wi separate beds o the metal tube kind like hospital beds. The bedrooms had plesterboard coved ceilins but ae lad accidentally pit his fit through the ceilin at Balkeerie and pasted a coloured picter ower it tae hide the hole. Sir Thomas liked tae inspect the place himsel and see hoo abody wis. So ae day he spots the picter on the ceilin and speirs foo it wis there. So the chap tells him it wis fine tae look at fan ye were lyin back in the bed. Sir Thomas himsel then lies doon on the bed tae see for himsel and agrees! Mackie o the Bent near Laurencekirk wis anither fermin pioneer and he had twa hostels there, een for sixteen men and een for ten dairymaids. A few bothies were improved eftir the war, wi electric licht and inside mains watter, but otherwise the same as afore. Only the odd eens like at Benshie, Findowrie and Pitgarvie were upgraded tae hostels.

Meat

THERE WAS A DIFFERENT SYSTEM in the north o the Mearns. Ye had a wee bothy wi a fireplace tae bide in, but got yere meat in the hoose. At Dillavaird abuin Auchenblae it was aye brose in the mornin, soup then boilin beef and tatties tae yere denner, and for yere tea as muckle hame-made bannocks and cheese as ye cud eat, but only *ae* slice o white loaf-breid, nae mair, it had tae be bocht in! Of coorse ye got less pey if ye got yere meat in the hoose. At Tannachie abuin Skite, the loun and the cattler got their meat in the hoose; a three coorse denner and a cooked tea, but the ither lads in the bothy made their ain meat. In Aberdeenshire it wis near a' meat in the hoose but it wis a lottery, at ae place ye got bra meat, as guid's the fermer, but ither places were fell scrapehard: brose in the mornin; tatties and skirlie wi yirned milk eftir for a puddin, for yere denner;

and sowens or porridge tae yere supper, and ye were sent oot o the kitchen tae a cald chaumer eftir 9 o'clock. In the bothy ye had tae mak yere ain meat but ye cud plaise yersel fan ye gaed tae yere bed. Breakfast was aye porridge, if there was nae loun or orraman in the bothy the horseman took week aboot tae mak them and the ither lads sa till their horse until they were made and abody in the bothy supplied the meal week aboot. As pairt o yere fee ye got a firlot (35 lb) o meal every month but ye selt half o it tae the baker for breid and ither things and ye got a chopin can o fresh unskimmed milk ilkey mornin, maybe a bittie less in winter. Some places ye got as muckle milk mornin and nicht, mair than ye needed. Some places in the Mearns gied the bothy lads a tattie allowance tae, but that was never the case in Angus. Ye cud aye get tatties though, some places lat ye tak some openly, especially at tattie hairst or dressin time, or auld tatties, but at ither times and places ye gaed oot at nicht and *libbed* the new tatties fae the dreel, laivin the sha's stannin.

Tae mak the porridge ye first bigget a great fire tae bring the watter tae the boil then trickled in handfu's o meal. If ye jist threw the meal in onywye ye wid get great dry knots or "*djeuk's heids*" in them. If they were badly made wi great dry knots amuin wattery brui they were said tae be "*a' knots and brui like bishop's shite*". Ae loun in his first week in the bothy at Reidhall in 1921 had never made porridge at hame and made a puir job, so the foreman spat the knots in his face until, eftir a week, he made them richt. The porridge was made in a muckle three-leggit pot that hung fae a swey ower the fire, there was sae muckle porridge it took a lang time tae cuil so whiles it was pit oot the bothy door tae sit a whiley. At Ethie Mains the laird's wife kept fancy djeuks. They were fund ae day peckin awa at the bothy porridge pot, so some o them 'disappeared', a cheenge frae brose for supper! At Benshie ae chap pit his bowel fu o porridge ootside the bothy door and een o the few cars aboot, a baby Austin, cam by and hit it. The bowel broke in twa but it was mid-term and he widna buy anither een. So he jist tied it ticht roond the boddam wi binder twine tae haud it thegither, and gin the end o the term it wis like a mavie's nest, barkit inside and oot!

At ae time the bothy lads et wi a horn spuin oot o a widden caup but gin later times, aroond 1930, it was only some o the alder lads that had them. They were cleaned be pitten them on the knee o their cord breeks and gien them a twist. In later times ye had a white cheena bowel like a big sugar bowel, and a metal spuin. Ye held the bowel be the flange at the boddam. If ye pit yere thoom ower the rim o the bowel ye wid get an affa rap ower the finger wi anither lad's spuin. Ye jist werna supposed tae haud yere bowel that wye, and that's a' there wis aboot it, jist like ye didna ging tae the coort athoot yere bonnet on. Anither thing was ye werna allowed tae wash yere bowel ower offen so it grew a rim o dried porridge and brose inside and was black wi dirty fingermarks ootside. It depended on the senior lad in the bothy hoo offen ye were allooed tae wash it. Sometimes it got washed every month but maistly only at the end o a sixmonth. If ye did wash it offener than the ither lads thocht ye sud, they wid brak it! The only ither time ye cud wash it wis fan ye had visitors fae anither bothy in for a game o cairds, so ye cud gie them tea. Ye et yere porridge, brose or stovies, and drank yere tea oot o the same bowel, ye had nae cup or jug. Ye jist gied it a sweel oot wi het watter or tea, threw this intae the aisle-hole aneth the fire, then poored yere tea. Ye had nae plate or fork aither, jist a knife for spreadin pieces and cuttin yere haffie. If ye were eatin eggs or sassages ye jist stuck them atween twa slices o haffie and et them that wye.

Denner in the summer wis offen *calders*, cald porridge left ower fae mornin. Ye filled yere bowel in the mornin and pit it inside yere mealer. Naebody here ever filled a dra'er wi porridge, there wisna sic a thing as a dra'er in the bothy. Some lads liket calders fine in the warm weather wi the craim fae the tap o the milk, ithers cudna thole them ava. Calders warmed up wi het milk wis ca'd *potty porridge*, they were that thick it wis said thet ye cud eat them oot o a hake! Some lads aiven fried slices o porridge. Itherwise ye micht hae a bit haffie and cheese and a cup o tea. In winter some made brose. Peasemeal brose wisna sae popular as in the north, some fowk said it was like caffie's skitter. Ye cud mak brose wi half oatmeal and half peasemeal, some lads ca'd that *lime and earth*. Ithers made a kind o steepies wi dry breid, meal and het milk and ca'd that *lime and earth* as it minded them o the squares o lime ye had tae brack up and mix wi earth on the fields. For variety ye cud boil a neep and yaise the brui tae mak brose and syne mash the neep and eat it eftir. Whiles some lads made a puddin wi *cremola* custard pooder and sugar be poorin on het milk and steerin it jist like brose.

Tea cud be jist a piece and jam or seerup, treckle wisna offen bocht for ye cud aye tak some calfie's treckle for yere piece. Ye micht hae a boilin o tatties, or mak stovies if there wis ony creesh in the pan fae the Sunday sassages, or ye cud mak *creeshie meallie* or *skirlie* as some fowk ca it, but ye needed an ingan fae some married lad's gairden. For a trait on baker's nicht ye micht hae haen a pie or a bridie. If a fishwife cam roond ye micht buy *ranns*, because they were cooked already. Ye cud aye get eggs, they were aye boiled or fried, ye jist pit them atween twa bits o haffie. Hens lay in mid-mornin so fan ye cam back tae the stable at denner time ye cud aye find some laid aroond the stable or steadin or aneth stacks unless the wifie had managed tae find them a', but the hens laid a' ower the place. It wisna stealin, maybe the hens belanged tae the fermer's wife, but the eggs belanged tae fa ever fund them. If there were djeuks ye gaed oot in the mornin, as they lay first thing. At Mains o Fettercairn there were swans in the mill-dam so if ye were lucky ye micht hae gotten a swan's egg. Of coorse ye cud collect peesie's or pictairnie's eggs tae eat or tae sell. Sunday breakfast was special. Ye took week aboot tae buy sassages for abody in the bothy, they were 1/— a pund afore the war.

> For beef wis ne'er in ower oor door
> But jist a pund at Yule sir

The only beef ye ever sa was on the huif, unless ye were helpin at anither ferm at a big threshin, fan the traivelin mill cam roond. Fermers wid lend a neighbour maybe three lads for three days and got the same help fan it cam roond tae him. Ye didna get onything fan ye were workin far ye were feed, only if ye were awa at anither ferm. Then ye got a midser piece at the mornin yokin. Sometimes jist a cookie or saftie and jam and a cup o tea, or ye micht get a bridie and a bottle o beer, Lochside Ale fae Montrose maybe. Ye aye got a bra denner in the fermhoose: broth then boilin beef or maybe stew or mince and tatties then a milk puddin or clootie dumplin. At hairst ye seldom got onything, a few places gied ye a midser piece. At Langbank aside Kirrie twa maids brocht denner oot tae the field. Fan een o the merried lads killed a pig the bothy lads whiles got invited for a feed, or at least ye got some fresh lard for makin stovies or creeshie meallie.

It wisna offen onybody did muckle cookin in the bothy, aiven at nicht fan ye had mair time. Ye cud get rabbits aisy eneuch but it wisna offen onybody bathered tae cook them. But abody kens the story aboot the fermer seekin a lost hen speirin at the bothy lads *"fat's that in yere pot the nicht"* and the chap sayin *"weel fermer, it gaed in a rabbit, it can come oot fat it likes".* Apairt fae yere milk and meal ye got as pairt o yere fee and ony eggs and tatties ye cud get yere hands on, ye had tae buy onything else fae the baker's vans that cam roond twice a week. The drivers worked affa lang oors, they whiles didna feenish their roond until 10 or 11 at nicht. The main things ye bocht aff the van wis a haffie o white loaf-breid, hard reid cheese, jam, seerup or treckle, tea, sugar and margarine, never butter, hit wis ower dear. If ye were affa lucky, and on guid terms wi the maid ye micht whiles get a bittie butter in yere milk can. For a trait ye micht buy a pie or a bridie, or a sma tin o bully beef for yere Sunday denner if it wis yere week tae bide ahent tae look eftir the horse, but ye didna hae the money tae buy ony *puffie-tooties.* Some lads mithers micht send a biscuit tin fu o hame-made bannocks and a twa pund jar o hame-made jam roond wi the baker's van, but abody wisna that lucky. On van day ye left a wee bookie on yere mealer wi a list o fat ye wanted and the baker wid set it on the kist and ye peyed him at the end o the month fan ye got yere *kick* aff yere sixmonth pey fae the fermer. It wis a' guid halesome farin if no very fancy, but hardly onybody wis ever seek and louns grew intae fine strappin men fit tae dae mony a hard day's wark on it. Ye had plenty o fresh milk and a wee bit variety noo and again and that kept maist fowk hale and hearty.

Bothy life was roch and ready at ony time but some lads liked tae joke that it wis coorser than fat it wis. Abody fae Eassie tae Fetterie kens aboot the *Bold Fearn* (Jim Fearn). He pretendit tae eat worms and young mice, some say that he did eat them, but it wis jist a bothy joke that he eence made stovies wi rats and cried *"dig deeper lads, there's beef in the boddam"*. Anither lad stories were telt aboot wis *Roch Annan*. Accordin tae ae story a young loun in the bothy said *"far I come fae we like oor tatties chappit"*. So *Roch Annan* couped the tatties on the flair, syne chapped them wi his shairny buits, so the loun et his tatties hale efter that!

Claes

IN THE BOTHY YE KEPT YERE CLAES in a kist aboot fower feet lang, yere workin claes cud lie aboot on the bed or hing on a hook but ye aye kept yere guid claes in yere claeser. Ye didna wear a semmit but a blue-grey flannel sark next yere skin. It had three or fower buttons at the neck and gaed on ower yere heid, and had lang tails back and front tae keep ye warm. It absorbed sweyt like a dress cotton sark widna. Workin ootside maist o the time ye cud be sweytin wi effort ae meenit and stairvin o cald the next fan the wind blew. Ye slept a' week in this sark tae, naebody in the bothy ever had a nichtgoon or pyjamas. Ower the tap o this sark ye wore anither thick woolen sark, Kircaldy strippet sarks had been the thing at ae time, later a checket or Irish tweed sark, whiles lined wi cotton. They gaed on ower yere heid and had lang tails as weel. Aneth yere breeks ye wore lang flannel drawers summer and winter. They had loops tae haud them up that looped aroond yere galluses. In winter ye wore heavy broon cord breeks. They had sterch in them, and fan they were new ye cud hardly bend yere knees wi them on, and if they got weet and dried oot, they cud stand up be theirsel! They were *never* washed, ye jist threw them awa fan they were duin. They had a slight flare fae the knee doon, thick saims and a pooch for yere watch, as ye didna wear a weystcoat fan ye were plooin:

> Ticht at the knee
> Sprung at the fit
> A raised saim
> And a watch pooch

In summer ye wore thick dark grey *moleskin* breeks like bobbies' breeks. Yere breeks were held up wi galluses aboot 2½ tae 3 inch wide. Ye wore *wull tams* buckled alow yere knees, no jist tae keep the boddam o yere breeks oot amuin gutters or shairn, but tae support the wecht o yere breeks and mak them mair comfortable tae wear. If ye were daen clorty wark ye tied sackin roond the fit o yere breeks wi binder twine. The wull tams were made at the saidlers, black leather wi white metal buckles. Roonded buckles were best, the square eens were like tae tickle intae things. Fan ye were workin ootside, as ye were maist o the time, ye wore a louse dungaree jaiket ca'd a *slop* or *greaser*, some fowk, especially aroond Kirrie wye, ca'd it a *kerseckie*. This wisna buttoned up unless it wis affa cald as ye needed freedom tae move. Ye micht wear an auld jaicket or weystcoat for the cauld but no buttoned unless ye were at an inside job, sittin at the thresher, but no for pu'in neeps or spreadin dung. On yere heid ye aye wore a checkit cloth bonnet, whiles ca'd a *doolichter*, as they were eence that broad it wis said that a doo cud licht on een. Some lads aroond the time o the First War yaised tae pit a cane inside the tap tae mak it stick oot a' the mair. On yere feet ye wore woolen socks, hame-knitted were the best, and heavy tacketty buits wi heel and tae rings wi a richt cant at the taes. Ye cud buy chaip factory-made buits for £1 or 22/6d, but ye were aye better tae spend £3 on a guid pair made for ye, aiven supposin that wis near three weeks pey, since they wid gie ye mair comfort and lested a lot langer, so they were chaiper in the lang run.

If ye were gaen oot at nicht ye took aff yere upper sark and pit on a white *bicycle sark* on tap o yere grey flannel sark. Sometimes ye pit the bicycle sark on tap o baith sarks. Some lads micht aiven wear fower sarks, and toonsfowk wondered foo ye cud stand a' nicht at the neuk and nae feel the cald! The bicycle sark got its name because ye aye pit it on afore bikin intae the toon. Some fowk in Angus ca'd it their *'Bertie Smairt'* eftir a great biker fae Baldoukie fa won bike races on a *Killacky* bike made in Forfar. Through the week ye had yere *scorgie* or *scuddlin* claes for second best, maybe a jaiket, weystcoat and breeks that didna match. For best ye wore a blue, or broon, three piece serge suit, yere guid bonnet, polished dress buits and a pocket watch and chain. The suits cost five guineas, aboot five weeks wages afore the war, but naebody stinted on their best claes. Even wi yere best claes for gaen oot on Setterday nicht ye didna wear a collar nor tie unless ye were coortin and tryin tae impress the dame's mither. If ye were jist gaen oot wi the ither lads and pit a tie on, they wid say *"yere nae comin wi us, yere ower toffed up"*.

The war affected claes, bib and brace dungarees began tae be worn ower workin breeks. Twa-piece suits cam in, even if ye had the money, ye didna aye hae the claithin coupons. Ye needed 21 for a twa-piece suit; 11 for the breeks and 10 for the jaicket but anither 5 for a weystcoat. Some lads wore shuin for dress afore the war but it became mair common eftir the war, but some lads aye preferred buits.

Jist as the bakers' vans cam roond wi breid and groceries so drapers and dealers biket roond ferms tae sell odds and ends. Sharples fae Bridge Street in Brechin cam roond wi a suitcase on his bike sellin chaip watches, threid, batchelors, or bulldog buttons (they needed nae shewin), collar studs etc. Ingersoll watches were 3/6d each and chaiper tae throw awa than sort; *"an Angeramasoll watch, guaranteed tae ging in ony country, if it winna ging ye can cairry it"*. Maist lads had guid watches costin £3 tae £5, at a time fan yere week's wages wis aboot £1. Anither bicycle salesman, fae Union Street, Brechin wis ca'd *Fly By Nicht*. He selt sma items like bicycle sarks, socks, chaip buits, and frenchies. There wis anither dealer ca'd *Harry the Jew*, a wee jewish-lookin mannie fae Montrose. He biket as far as Eassie, Glamis and Kirrie, dealin in watches, offerin tae buy gold watches and sellin chaip eens. Ye had traivelin photographers comin roond tae, so ye micht a pose a' thegither, somebody cuttin a haffie wi an aixe, a besom hanle or a sheepstake tae steer the porridge pot or an auld washin-hoose boiler for a caper, or wi fiddles, melodians and pipes, whether ye cud play them or no. Or ye pit on yere guid claes tae get yere photo taen wi yere pair, a' weel turned oot.

Fun and games

IN THE WINTER it wis dark early so ye amused yersel in the bothy maist nichts. Ye spent some nichts jist polishin yere horse harness. Naebody read books, jist weekly papers like the *People's Journal* or the *Weekly News*, the bothy had a puir licht, ye wid hae strained yere eeen readin ower muckle. Maistly ye played cairds: *nap, stop the bus, or catch the ten* but maistly *nap*. Whiles ye micht hae lads ower fae anither bothy for a game o cairds so ye made a pot o tatties or stovies and a cup o tea for the visitors. Dominoes and drafts wis popular tae. Or ye had daft games like *sweir tree*: twa o ye sat on the flair wi the soles o yere buits thegither and ye baith grippet a besom shaft and tried tae be first tae pu the ither lad up aff the flair. Anither caper wis: some lad held ye be the legs and ye walked on yere hands grippin buit brushes and then tried tae pick up pennies fae the flair wi yere teeth. Radios, or wirelesses as they were ca'd, were very rare afore the war. Apairt fae the expence o buyin een ye needed tae tak the weet batteries tae a shop tae get them rechairged every sae offen. Even wee wind-up gramophones were seldom seen in the bothy but there wis near aye some lad that cud play the trump or the moothie or aiven a melodian, or the fiddle or pipes, or cud sing cornkisters. It wis a' Scottish music of coorse, some lads were able tae play a tune o some sort, ithers were real guid musicians and micht tak lessons fae somebody like Jim Cameron fae Kirrie. He wis eence a bothy lad himsel, and wis a plooin champion as weel's a champion fiddler afore he had a dance band. A great mony dance band musicians started oot in the bothy, in fact maybe the maist o them did:

> Fan wark is ower and supper duin,
> Oor bothy band comes on the scene,
> At jigs, strathspeys and highland reels,
> There's few can beat oor bothy chiels.

In summer ye had lang lichty nichts and mair time tae yersel fan the horse were oot on grass and didna need tae be fed or muckit oot. Ye played ootside games and sports: throwin the hammer, tossin the caber, or throwin a 56 lb weicht ower a line were a' popular, as wis quoits. Ye didna hae richt-like quoits, jist muckle horse-shuin. An iren spike wis hammered intae the grund, and then a pit wis dug in front o't and the earth wis mixed wi watter tae mak sticky mud so's the horshae wid stick far it landed. The een nearest the pin won. Fitba of coorse wis aye affa popular, aither jist a kick aboot atween twa bothies wi jaickets for goalposts, or whiles proper teams; Balwyllo Amateur F.C. is still on the go, and yaises pairt o the auld bothy for a clubhoose. Rural men's clubs were started up in the 1920s, offen be the dominie or the meenister in the first place. Some fermers werna in favour o clubs, but there wis naething they cud dae aboot it. They didna like the men tae organise or think for theirsel, aiven for fun. The men's clubs organised sports and whist drives and dances alang wi the W.R.I.s. Socials were held in the local schuil if there wis nae parish hall.

There were een or twa annual events ye took pairt in, but Christmas wisna een o them, hit wis jist anither workin day, but of coorse abody gaed first fittin at New Year and ye got the day aff. Awa back Halla'even wis celebrated and fowk were whiles sae late wanderin aboot guisin it wis near time tae yoke gin the time they got hame. Ae chap eence gaed guisin wearin his lang dra'ers, a lum hat and a auld cla hemmer jaiket, but got hame sae late he had tae ploo like that the next mornin! The Taranty Market aside Brechin was a great event every June. Fowk biket fae a' ower Angus and the Howe o the Mearns tae ging tae it. Some hardy ploomen wid hae a go at the booth boxers but it wisna offen they cud beat them, they a' had nesty tricks, it wisna exactly Marquis o Queensberry rules. The Toon Cooncil held coort in a hoose aside the muir and onybody gettin oot o hand wis fined on the spot or spend a nicht in the cells. Ye wid get the efternuin aff for the local show, like the Fetterie show, aye held on a Wednesday.

On Setterdays ye maistly biket intae the nearest toon. Afore the war it cost ye 4d or 6d tae get intae the picters. Lowrnie had a picter hoose as weel's the bigger toons, far there wis twa or three. If ye gaed tae the pub it cost ye 1/1d for a nip and a pint. There were aye dances on a Setterday nicht. At places like the Temperance Hall in Brechin there were aye Scottish music and dances, there micht be a waltz or a polka but it wis maistly Scottish. They were kent as ploomen's dances, it wis maistly country lads and lassies that gaed tae them. There wis a shortage o lassies on the ferm. There wis offen only ae maid in the fermhoose and fower or mair young lads in the bothy. A lot o country lassies worked as maids tae doctors, solicitors, meenisters and sic weel aff fowk in the toons. They only got ae nicht aff in the middle o the week, maybe Wednesday or Thursday. So the bothy lads gaed intae the toon on the maids' nicht aff. This was ca'd *dame nicht* or *moll nicht* or the *nicht o the three Rs* (razzer, rum and ride).

Fan ye did ging intae the toon ye cud laive yere bike at een o the bike shops for 2d for safekeepin. The bikes maistly had carbide lamps, it cost 2d for a refill. Earlier there had been reekin paraffin lamps wi a puir licht like a spark in the mist. Gin the 1930s some lads had motor bikes, petrol then cost 1/— a gallon. Durin the war it wis difficult tae get petrol but if ye kent somebody that had a petrol allowance for startin paraffin tractors (they aye got far mair than fat they needed), ye were in luck. But then they started pittin reid colourin in it. Ye cud filter it so ye cud run yere bike on it, but it took oors. If ye did get yere hands on petrol, tae avoid suspeeshin fae the bobbies ye micht laive yere bike somewye safe and walk intae toon.

The pubs closed at 10 p.m. in summer and 9.30 p.m. in winter. Afore ye set aff hame ye cud hae a fish supper for 4d or a *tiger* for 2d. A tiger wis jist a piece made wi slice o bully beef.

Valentine's shoppie aside Duncan's bike shop in Brechin was ae place that selt *tigers*. Ither shoppies selt hough or het tripe and bannocks. In Forfar the bridie shops were whiles open fan the dances feenished. If it wis yere turn tae buy the sassages for Sunday mornin ye cud buy them on the wye hame if ye gaed tae a *midnicht butcher*, they bade open eftir the pubs closed jist for the bothy lads. So that wis yere Setterday nicht oot, ye collected yere bike and awa hame tae yere bothy, maybe ten mile or mair. Naebody thocht onything aboot that. Some lads even biket aboot 25 mile tae Dundee tae see Scott Skinner dae a concert, then bike hame in the dark.

Practical jokes were aye a favourite ploy wi the bothy lads. A common caper wis tae pit a divot on a bothy lum and tie the door shut tae reek fowk oot. Jockie Elrick had a bump on his heid like an egg a' his days fae a bothy door shuttin on his heid fan he wis tryin tae win oot. A new merried couple wid get reekit oot o their hoose the same wye. There were lots o other capers. If a bothy lad was coortin the maid on the same ferm his kist wid be cairried awa tae anither bothy. Ae chap at Benshie wis bet that he cudna run tae the tap o a snadrift. He wis in his sark tails and bare feet, ready tae gae awa tae his bed. So, of coorse the meenit he wis oot o the bothy the door wis barred shut. So he spent the nicht in the hey laft for warmth, but wis eaten a' ower be mites. The loun cud aye expect a bit o daidlin, although the heid lad in the bothy, if he had ony sense, never lat it get oot o hand. The loun cud aye expect *cock dreel*: some lad grabbed ye atween the legs and garred ye loup aff the flair ower the pot or on tae a kist and so on. Or, if the loun was left ahent fan the ither lads gaed awa tae the pub, fan they cam back they micht slide the shepherd's libbin knife up his bare leg (him lyin in his bed) until he cam oot in a cald sweyt for fear o losin his future mairrage prospects. There were some tragic stories that abody repeated, some said they happened at sic and sic a place, some anither place, but they micht hae happened afore the First War. The best kent een was aboot a chap tied tae the bothy form and left himsel. The form coupit in front o the fire fan he tried tae win free and he wis burnt tae death. Anither tale was aboot a chap tied in a poke and left at the roadside. Some lad passin got sic a fleg fan a sound cam fae the poke that he struck it wi a plooshare, and killed the puir chap in the poke. Naebody had ever seen ony o this wi there ain een but the stories were repeated as a kind o a warnin no tae lat bothy capers get ower roch.

On a Sunday, eftir yere sassage and egg breakfast, unless it wis yere week tae bide ahent and see tae the horse, ye biket hame wi yere washin. If ye were ower far fae hame ye had tae pey some wifie tae dae it for ye.

> *The plooman's commandment*
> Six days shalt thou labour
> And do all that thou art able
> On the Sabbath day wash the horses' legs
> And tidy up the stable

Feein time

THERE WERE FEEIN MERCATS in a' the toons in the district and at Friock. The term times were at Whitsunday, the 28th o Mey; and Mertinmas, the 28th o November. Ye loused at dennertime on the 28th and ye had up tae three days tae get a fee. If athing on the ferm was weel aheid be term time ye micht hae gotten aff a day or twa early. Forfar and Lowrnie were on Monday, Brechin and Dundee on a Tuesday, Friock and Steenhyve on Thursday, Montrose and Aiberdeen's Muckle Market on Setterday. Forfar wis ca'd the *rogues market*, onybody that cudna got a fee gaed there. The feein mercats were held on the same day as the cattle mert except at Friock, it had nae mert. The married lads feed eence a year at the Mey term, except at Dundee far it wis at the winter term. The single lads feed every sixmonth, aiven if ye liked a place it was a point o honour nae tae bide ony langer than twa terms, unless ye got promotion, or ye were jist a stick in the mud, nae man ava. Ither times ye were fell gled tae win awa for a cheenge. Ye micht pit a cloot on a bit stick, or *flag* the bothy lum, tae lat abody ye were gaen:

The term time is near at hand
And I'll suin be laivin
I've flagged the bothy lum
Tae show that I'm nae grievin
For its the helluva'st mess o gutters I ever sa
I wis' it wis the term and lat's awa

The fermers near aye gaed tae the nearest mert but lads seekin a new fee wid traivel aboot tae different eens if they thocht there wis a better chance o gettin on. Ye aye tried tae get a better pair, if ye had been orrabaister as loun ye tried tae get on for a pair, and if ye'd haen a pair ye tried tae get on for second or foreman, dependin on fat pair ye'd haen at yere lest place. Ye wid hing aboot near the mert or the pubs and hotels the fermers gaithered. At Friock ye lined up alang Gardyne Street wi a strae in yere moo if ye hadna gotten a fee. Ye aye waited til a fermer speired if ye were seekin a fee. Some fermers had a bad name, so ye widna fee wi them if ye kent ony ill aboot them:

Its a flowin pot at the Mains o Dun
But hackin sticks at Balwyllo

There wis a story fae the time Fetterie had a feein mercat. A fermer speired at a loun if he wis seekin a fee, the loun says aye. So the fermer gaed on tae speir fa his lest employer had been and gaed awa tae see him and cam back and says tae the loun *"Weel lathie, I've been speirin aboot ye an' I'm tae tak ye"*. But the loun says *"And I've been speirin aboot you and I'm nae gaen"*. Anither time, at Brechin, Jocky Johnstone fae Bonnybreich speirs at a lad if he'd gotten a fee. He says *"Aye, West Kintrockat"* and Jockie says *"Huh, its nae muckle better"*. In 1921 a loun was offered £20 for a sixmonth first fee and 1/— arles, £21 if he did weel! Aroond 1928 an orrabaister micht get £26 and 2/6 arles. In the 1930s a 5th horseman got £38 for a sixmonth and jist afore the war arles were up tae 5/— fae some fermers. Ye arranged wi the fermer foo muckle o a monthly *kick* ye wanted as an advance on yere wages, and at the end o the term, wi ony luck ye micht hae a pound or twa coming tae ye.

Eftir the war weekly wages were aboot £3 tae £3.10/— aroond 1955, and gin 1964 £10.10/— tae £11.

The farrer sooth ye gaed the wages were generally better so Angus lads wid ging tae Perthshire and Mearns lads cam intae Angus. Some fermers were affa greedy and gaed tae an agency run be a wifie in Aiberdeen tae get north lads on the chaip. They offen cam doon intae the Howe o the Mearns and then intae Angus and if they bade twa terms they never gaed north again. They werna aye popular as they kept wages doon here as they were yaised tae sma'er wages up north and undercut the local lads. Although they were guid aneuch horsemen, they cudna big a stack. Ye see they were yaised wi different wyes o workin up north. They had wee *ricks* as they ca'd them, bigget on a cobbled foond wi a layer o bruim and branches, nae stachels, nae like oors ava. Their first fee doon here offen wasna worth the fermer's while until they got intae oor wye o workin. If ye said tae some north lad *"awa ye heilant bugger, ye jist come doon here tae tak a white man's livin"* he micht say *"fit the hell colour dae ye think I am?"* Some Angus lads wid aiven admit that the Perthshire lads were better than them at some jobs, the farrer sooth ye gaed the mair sheaves there were in a stook and the bigger the stacks:

> North for kye and weemen
> Sooth for men and horse

If the fermer ye'd been workin for speired if ye wid bide on and get on fae third tae second pair ye micht say *"weel I'll bide on for second wi ye if I can keep the pair I hiv, I've got them weel trained"* and if he said no ye wid say *"Awa tae hell wi ye than, I'm nae bidin"*. Ye micht be back at the same place eftir a few terms or even mair than eence, as lang as ye got yere pey up. If ye agreed wi a fermer tae ging wi him for a term it wis purely a verbal contract, ye got yere arles and like the King's shillin, that bound ye tae the agreement. Ye micht get tae a place tae find that abody else had cleared oot, seein it wis sic an affa like place, so ye wid work an oor or twa tae pey aff yere arles and clear oot tae. If ye'd ony money left at feein time ye had a drink or twa and a guid denner. Feein time wis the only holidays ye ever got except New Year's Day, or ye micht get tae the local show in summer, so ye made the maist o't. The fermer ye were tae ging tae sent a cairt ower tae yere auld place tae pick up yere kists, ye had them a' labelled and tied up, or they cud be sent be rail dependin on foo far ye were movin. Fae the 1930s the cairriers larry wis sometimes sent or there were taxies fitted up tae cairry kists.

In late 1940 the government brocht in a guaranteed minimum wage and the *standstill order* tae stop the system o movin every sixmonth. It maybe geid some fowk better wages but it didna plaise abody. If ye thocht yersel mair skilled ye cudna move tae get yere wages up, but the fermers cud still get rid o onybody they didna want. Some lads were that raised aboot this system they were willin tae ging "*doon the Howe*" tae Perth prison, maist were fined. This wartime restriction wis kept on a guid while eftir the war be the Labour government. Lang eftir the war wis ower lads were still bein fined for movin. It seems tae hae been the Tories that did awa wi this in the 1950s, though there wis still a guaranteed minimum wage. Some young lads started tae move aboot every sixer like afore the war, but ithers had got yaised tae bidin in ae place. If they did move it wis fae seein an advert in the front page o the *Courier*. The system o feein deid oot, though there were a few young bothy lads still gaein tae the merts at the auld term times. Married lads offen bade on the same place till they retired, far afore the war they shifted maist years.

If ye wanted awa fae ferm work athegither there werna mony options. Afore the war ye cud tak an *Irishman's rise* and ging on the railway track maintenance squads and get on for ganger if ye were lucky. Or ye micht drive coal horse in the toon, or get a job cairtin or labourin wi the cooncil. Yere skills, apairt fae drivin horse, werna muckle yaise in the toon. Eftir the war some lads back fae the forces widna ging back tae the bothy and took tae larry drivin, some gaed tae the Coonty Cooncil roads department, some tae the Hydro Board.

The term time is dra'in near
Fan we will win a fee
An' wi the *weary fermers
Again we'll never fee

*weary = miserable

Horse

CLYDESDALES WERE BRA ANIMALS tae work wi, maistly canny and willin and they got tae ken the job as weel's a man. Ye only got the odd een that was ill-gettit and wid kick or nip yere airm or crush ye in the sta, maybe because it had been ill-treated. Fan ye got yere ain pair tae look eftir and yoke, the three o ye cam thegither as a team. The horse were near a' bocht inn fae ootside the district, maist were bocht in fae the sooth, but some guid horse cam fae Aikey Fair. Chaip horse were bocht fae Blackie in Farfar. A few Belgians and Percherons were bocht in, heavy built horse, but they werna sae popular. Fermers that liked tae deal in horse employed a *staigger* tae brak in and train young horse or *staigs*. The staigs were bocht in as twa-year aulds and tae start wi they were yokit only tae pu a pole, jist tae get them yaised tae the harness and chains. They were first yokit tae a ploo be the staigger at the age o three but were worked gently, for a young horse cud burst its hert if it wis hashed. They were fit tae work at fower year auld but they were at their peak at aboot six tae eicht year auld. A horse that had been een o the first pair wid get handed doon tae second and third and sae on, as it got aulder and less fit. Gin the time they were twelve-year-auld maist horse were a bittie duin and wid be yokit as orrabaist, fit for lichter jobs like the tattie harra's or a licht cairtload. Some horse gaed on workin this wye as auld as 16 or aiven 22. The orrabaist wis offen worked be the loun, but thir auld horsies kent the routine better than the loun and needed nae tellin, they wid back intae the shafts withoot a word.

Geldins were preferred in this district, a few mares were yokit but they pish oot ahent, through their tails, and some horsemen didna like workin wi them. Tae the north and sooth mares and geldins were yokit thegither but hereaboots ye aye had twa mares or twa geldins. In the north they liket blind bridles, but here we liket the horse tae see oot a' roond. A pair o horse was needed tae work every 80 acre on a ferm, or onything fae 60 tae 90 acre. They aye had short names, aisier for the horse tae follow its orders: geldins had names like Jip, Jock, Star, Brisk, Dan, Ben, Bob, King, York, Clyde or Paddy; mares had names like Nell, Bess, Jean, Meg, Bell or Nan.

The main words o command were: *hey* for left turn, *wheesh* for richt turn, *woah* for stop and *tck-tck* (wi yere tougue ahent yere teeth) for go. If ye got a horse trained ootside the district it micht be yaised tae ither commands. Ye aye spoke tae yere pair tae encourage them, "*come on noo*", "*guid lad*" and so on. Ye kept yere steadiest horse on the left fan ye were plooin, yere *hander* and yaised it tae control the ither een. Fan ye were cairtin ye wid maistly pit yere *hander* atween the shafts as yere *cairter* and yere second horse in the thaits as yere *thaiter* but ye cheenged them aroond noo and again. Fan ye were comin hame at nicht ye rode yere *hander* and led the second horse wi a tow on the richt hand side o the road, like a pedestrian.

Ye aye liked yere horse and harness lookin weel, aiven supposin yere workin claes were orra. Ye had a best harness for gaen intae toon and an achday harness for workin in the field. Some lads had their ain haims, back chains and ither bits o harness, kept clean wrapped in a seck. Ye liked yere pair tae look weel gaen intae toon. Some lads had decorations that jingled as the horse moved. They werena as fancy as show harness though, jist for a bit swank fan fowk were like tae see ye. Tae get the leather bonny it wis washed then rubbed wi bleck and beeswax, as mony as six coats, rubbed in wi a *beetle*, a specially shaped widden stick, then feenished aff wi a duster. The fermers gied ye chaip bleck whiles, but Jamieson's bleck wis the best. The metal pairts were cleaned wi emery paper. The chains ye pit in a juit poke filled wi sand and sa'dust, hooked at ae end tae the trevis o yere horse sta and then ye walloped it for as lang as twa oors if ye had the strength, or ye peyed a young loun tae dae it for ye. Ye cud yaise newspaper tae, ye stuffed as muckle paper intae the poke as ye cud, and walloped it the same as wi sand.

In the mornin ye mucked oot yere pair and pit doon clean strae beddin. Moss litter wis bra stuff for beddin if ye got it. It cam in bales held thegither wi wire and straps o wid that made handy kindlin. A layer o moss litter jist needed a rake up ilkae day and lested a week. Ye groomed yere pair mornin and nicht wi a dandy brush. It had a leather strap that gaed ower the back o yere hand. The foreman maisered oot wi a scull the allo'ance o bruised corn for ilkae horse. The corn wis held in a fireclay troch in the manger. The horse were fed corn and hey in the mornin. If the hey laft wis abuin the stable the hey wis forket doon intae the hake, but it wis better if ye pit it in the manger as it wis like tae fae doon fae the hake and spoil yere efforts at groomin. Ye then geid them watter. At denner time ye wattered them as suin as ye loused, and they got a feed o corn and a neep or some cattle cake as a wee trait. They were wattered again at nicht and then fed and groomed again. Aboot eicht at nicht ye looked in tae see that they were a' richt and maybe geid them a neep. Fan ye were a horseman ye spent maist o yere workin day wi yere pair and ye got tae like the willin, intelligent beasts. Nae self-respectin horseman wid ever lat onybody, includin a fermer illtrait horse, and say or dae naething aboot it, aiven if it meant lossin yere job. Ye had ower muckle likin and respect for the horse tae see ony hairm duin tae them.

Ye cud play tricks on fowk wi horse though. If some foreman wis bla'in ower muckle aboot his pair ye cud rub the brechams wi rabbit's or pig's urine and he wid never get it ower the horse's neck. They were terrifeed at the smell o pigs especially. If the fermer had a new bocht staig some lads micht spend a' nicht brackin it in, so in the mornin the fermer and the staigger were fair amazed foo it took tae bein harnessed wi nae bather. Some lads that had special wyes wi horse cud spoil anither lad's horse at a plooin match wi jist a word, but at the risk o a thick lug if he was fund oot. Some lads had horse trained like circus horse tae react tae a single word, but nae abody had the *Horseman's Word* and nae aiven abody that had the *Word* had the same ability wi horse.

The daily darg and yearly roond

The plooman's week
Soor Monday
Cauld Tuesday
Cruel Wednesday
Everlastin Thursday
Oh Friday will ye ne'er gae duin
Sweet Setterday and the eftirnuin
Glorious Sunday rest forever
Amen

IF YE WERE A HORSEMAN ye had tae rise at 5 in the summer tae feed and muck oot yere horse, then back tae the bothy for yere porridge and tea and then yoke at 6.30 and work wi'oot a brack or 11 fan ye loused for twa oors. This wis for the horse's benefit, nae yours. Ye yoked again at een and loused at six. Yere horse were oot on grass in the summer so ye didna hae muckle tae dae afore ye got yere tea. In winter ye rose at 5.30 and yoked fae 7 tae 11.30, then 1 tae 5. Ye then had tae see tae yere horse so it wid be near 6 afore ye got yere tea. It wis dark fan ye yoked in the mornin and dark again fan ye loused at nicht. It helped ye tae see far ye were gaen if yere horse had white feet. A horse cud brack its shouder if the ploo struck a steen in frozen grund, but in winter the grund had tae be rock hard wi frost afore ye didna ploo. It had tae be sna'in blind-drift or rainin hale-watter afore the gaffer got ye an inside job makin strae raips or threshin.

Eftir the corn and tattie hairst maist o yere time wis spent plooin and harra'in. A seven year rotation wis yaisyil. Eftir tatties or neeps the grund wis plooed, then gaen across wi' the grubber, pu'ed be twa pair. Then it wis harra'ed ae wye, then the ither, and better than harra'ed then sawn wi winter wheat. The broadcaster wis six or seven yairds lang and made a rut in the grund so ye cud see clearly far ye'd sawn, and didna miss oot ony grund. It wis then harra'ed doon the same wye, then across. Then ye shut the gate till the followin August. Maist places grew wheat mainly for the strae which wis the best for throwin aff watter. It wis aye yaised for theekin stacks and happin tattie pits. The best o the grain of coorse wis selt for

53

millin, the seconds kept for hen's meat. If a ferm had fower fields o corn, it micht hae haen twa o barley and een o wheat. Grass seed was whiles sawn amuin wheat in the spring but it didna come up or the second year and wisna high aneuch tae get cut wi the grain the first year. It cam up the next summer, was left ley, then cut for hay the year eftir. It wis yaised for pasture the next year and got dunged be the cattle. At the end o that year it wis plooed up and corn sawn in April. Spreadin lime wis a nesty job, the squares o lime had tae be broken up and mixed wi earth. Ye tied sackin roond the boddam o yere breeks but some o the stoor aye got in and burned yere legs.

Neeps were pit in eftir corn. They needed a lot o wark, the corn stubble wis marked aff in six yaird squares be makin ruts in the grund. This wis the area a man wis supposed tae be able tae spread dung ower wi a graip. The dung wis cairted oot fae the coort and the midden and a haip wis pit in ilkae square eventually. The gaffer, orraman, loun and horseman a' spread dung but the horsemen took turn aboot cairtin, which gied them a brack. The cattler wid be graipin dung ontae the cairt so abody mucked in. This wis duin in October and November afore the end o the term. The dung wis then plooed in and left until spring. In spring dreels were made wi the dreel ploo, the neeps sawn and the dreels split again ower the seed wi the dreel ploo. Neeps had aye tae be in afore the term, Mey the 28th. The neeps *breered* aboot a fortnicht eftir so in mid-June abody was oot thegither wi the clatts (push-hyows) tae single the neeps, the horsemen a' in order: foreman, second, third etc., orraman and loun, then the gaffer and the cattler and whiles a dog followed the squad. Ye cud hae nine or ten fowk or mair, whiles weemen tae, a'hyowin. It wis een o the horsemen's least favourite jobs, a fell dreary ploy and nae horse work. But ye were a' workin thegither so ye got a chance tae crack. Like athing else ye took pride in makin a guid job. Ye picked oot the strongest lookin plants and pushed back and forrit wi the clatt gettin rid o the weeds and excess plants: *"push and pull and clean the dreel"*. The foreman set the pace, and if ithers wernae sae skilled they still had tae keep up, so some dreels wid be better duin than ithers. The dreels were then cleared oot wi the three-dreel neep

A studio photo of three Arrat ploomen around 1910. They wear
their three-piece suits with collarless "bicycle sarks" and no ties.
This was their usual walking-out gear, ties were only for special
occasions.

The well-dressed Arrat plooman, around 1930. Alf Birnie in his best Sunday claes. The small black diamond on his left sleeve commemorated the death of his sister. The bicycle has the usual carbide lamp.

The well-dressed Arrat plooman in 1956. Andy Church was
possibly the very last loun to leave school to live in a bothy and
work with horses in the district. Andy later worked in Fife and
Perthshire but returned to Arrat three times. When Arrat finally
gave up its horses in 1964 Andy went to work timber with horses
before joining his brother in dry stane dyking.

George Brandie with the Brechin United Co-operative Society "Soshie" van in the early 1930s. This was one of many bakers' vans which took bread and groceries around the bothies and cottar hooses. Such vanmen often finished their rounds as late as 11 p.m.

Opposite page

upper photograph
Newton of Guthrie bothy lads in 1930. A typical self-parodying posed photo with fiddles and bagpipes, the usual axe cutting a "haffie" and a bottle of beer. Behind can be seen a china bowl of the type used by then in place of the earlier wooden "caup". Milk cans can be seen in the foreground.

lower photograph
An unknown bothy group somewhere in Angus in the 1920s. A melodian this time, a bothy barber, the axe and "haffie", a bottle of beer and another common self-parody, the shovel of meal into an old boiler, stirred with a stick.

NWTON OF GUTHRIE . DEC. 1930.

upper photograph
Wull Knox, Chae Cruikshanks and Sy Riddler at Windyedge near
Brechin in the late 1920s. This photo shows the details of the grey
flannel sarks, heavy duty cords and galluses. The white loops
holding up their long flannel drawers can be seen looped around the
galluses. The trousers have a watch pooch on the right, Sy Riddler's
watch chain can be seen.

lower photograph
A threshing mill and traction engine belonging to the Brechin
contractors J. C. & W. Christie, around 1905. They operated over a
wide area of Angus and the Mearns until combine harvesters
rendered the travelling mills redundant by the 1960s.

Taranty smiddy near Brechin around 1900, an unusually elaborate
smiddy building dating from about 1860. Every estate had its
smiddy which was leased out with the understanding that all the
farms on the estate would resort to it to get their horses shod and
their implements repaired.

Hairst scene at Arrat in the 1960s, by then horse-drawn binders were a rare sicht in the area. Nine of the farm's ten horses are used here to draw the three binders.

opposite page

upper photograph
A neep-clattin squad at Hayston, Glamis in the 1930s,
photographed during a break. This wasn't a popular job with
horsemen, but they could smoke and swap yarns, a dog often
followed the squad. Note the loose "slops" or "greasers" worn,
usually only buttoned at the top.

lower photograph
Harry Cargill driving a Massie-Harris four-wheel-drive tractor
pulling a grubber. Behind it lies a grass-seed broadcaster, at
Birkenbush, Oathlaw. Such pre-war tractors with "spuds" on the
wheels were not allowed to go on public roads. To cross a metalled
road planks were put down, the "spuds" had to be removed in order
for them to travel along the roads. The early tractors were only used
for heavy work where three horses were needed, as with grubbers
and binders.

Jim Gibb with "his" pair around 1895. Jim was born in the 1870s
the son of a Glenesk shepherd. After working as a ploughman for a
time he later became a flockmaster, traversing the roads with a
flock of sheep between rented grazings. He wears a striped working
"Kircaldy" sark. By the 1920s it was customary to wear best suit
and bicycle sark for such photos, usually taken on a Sunday
morning. Blind bridles were not usual in the district but appear
here.

opposite page
A line-up of horses and horsemen at Arrat, near Brechin around
1910. The foreman and first pair are on the right, the fourth man
and pair to the left. The third man has one of the wide-brimmed
bonnets which came into fashion then, possibly with a cane inside
the top. At this time Arrat had "fower pair and an orra baist" but
later acquired a few more acres and had five pair.

Dave Alexander with a "110 Yank" plough at Cotton of
Kincaldrum, Inverarity around 1930. The horses have "doddie"
breachams rather than the usual pointed type, and the harness has
blinkers.

A typical four-man bothy at Newton of Stracathro. The inside was divided into a bedroom with two double caff beds and a kitchen with fireplace. This example backed on to the farmhouse garden.

Photo by the author

The bothy and cart-shed range at Mains of Glamis, all slated with local grey slate and possibly dating from 1840 or earlier. The bothy was one of the largest in the district, designed to accommodate eight men or boys. Inside were bare stone walls while later bothies had timber lining. There were four double caff beds upstairs, heated by a grill in the floor above the ground floor kitchen fireplace. Other large bothies, probably later than this, had a second fireplace upstairs. But this bothy had a pump at the door and an inside coal-hole, so was relatively sophisticated and was situated very close to the court and stable. The interior shows signs of having been occupied as late as around 1970.

Photo by the author

A tiny bothy which probably housed only two men, on the slopes of
Garvock at Forgie, Benholm Parish. Very unusually it is built of
brick rather than local stone.   *Photo by the author*

A small bothy built on the end of a cotter house at Milton of
Dillavaird, Glenbervie. In this area north of the Howe o' the Mearns
some or all of the single men usually got their "meat in the hoose"
(food in the farm kitchen) but spent their evenings in a bothy with a
fire, rather than in the farmhouse kitchen as in Aberdeenshire.
                                          Photo by the author

Farm staff with the maidies at Keithock around 1901–05. Two of
the men wear Boer War surplus bush hats and most wear
Kirkcaldy strippet sarks and wull tams. Contact with the maids on
the same farm was limited and the maids were not allowed inside
the bothy except when the men were away, but love usually found a
way.

harra's, pu'ed be ae horse, it wis licht and ye jist lifted it ower the end rigs. The neeps were singled again aboot a month later. The foreman or some ither lad micht come on a dreel badly duin the first time and cry oot *"fa the hell's dreel wis this?"* and there wid be a chorus *"It wisna mine"*.

The neep dreels were *shimmed* or horse-hoed twa or three times in the summer tae keep the weeds doon. Ye worked as close as ye cud tae the neeps withoot takin ony oot wi the weeds. The yella neeps were pu'ed in mid-October afore the warst frosts and were stored inside, but if they got *blasted* they were tapped and tailed wi yere *tapner* or turnip knife afore bein fed tae cattle. The sheep ate neeps aff the dreel but had their neeps hashed for them and pit intae trochs in the hardest weather. The swede neeps were a' the sweeter o bein frostit and cud be left in the dreel a' winter, and often werna a' pu'ed until Mey. They were jist pu'ed fan they were needed be the cattler, the gaffer, the orraman and the loun, a sair job if the grund wis hard wi frost. Ye cud fit an *angel* or *bonsagger* tae the front o a dreel ploo. This wis shaped like an arra'heid, it cut aff the lang ruits on twa dreels at a time athoot damagin the neeps, and made them a lot aisier tae pu. The last swedes wid be pu'ed and the grund plooed jist afore the Mey term.

Eftir the auld neep dreels were ploo'ed and harra'ed, barley wis sawn in late spring, jist afore the Mey term. If ye were harra'in in the affa dry weather ye offen get in spring, the stoor stuck tae the sweyt on the cheeks o yere erse and ye cud get a richt scadded doup. It wis like twa sheets o sandpaper rubbin thegither a' day and wis damned sair. Some lads stuck a sma pebble atween their cheeks tae stop them rubbin thegither, some aiven had a bittie polished wid the richt shape. The favourite joke cure was tae stick a young *teuchat* atween yere cheeks! Tatties like neeps needed tae be weel dunged and main crop varieties were planted in spring. Hey was cut aboot the end o June, eftir the *bloom* was aff as the pollen irritated the horse. If the mower needed sharpened at the smiddy this wis duin on a rainy day, the blades ye cud shairpen wi carborundum yersel, but the fingers had tae be taen tae the smiddy tae get buffed flush. The various types o hey rakes: tumlin tams, puddocks etc. were pu'ed by a single horse. The hey wis turned twa or three times tae dry aff ower aboot twelve workin days. If cut on Friday or Setterday mornin it wis turned on the Monday and be the Wednesday or Thursday pit intae coles aroond triangular widden bosses aboot seven or eicht feet high. The hey wis left in coles until jist afore the corn hairst. Then it wis taen in tae fill the hey laft or hey hoose and ony empty sta's in the stable, and the rest intae stacks. They were wider and no sae high as corn stacks but theekit wi wheat strae jist the same. Eftir the hey wis cut the field wis sawn wi clover and yaised for grazin sheep on. In atween heymakin, if it wis ower weet, ye wid be at the neep clattin.

The hairst lestit aboot six weeks fae mid-September intae October, a guid bittie later than nooadays. Ye were feed tae work fower Setterdays a' day and worked an extra oor every day durin the hairst. Corn wis cut first, then barley and then wheat, which took langest tae grow and ripen. The reaper-binders needed three horse tae pu them if they were workin on slopin grund. The gaffer said fa wis tae work them so as a' the horsemen got a turn. There were at least twa on maist ferms, whiles three or fower, offen een wis broken doon at ae time or anither. On sma placies the simpler and chaiper reaper wis yaised and the shaives had tae be tied be hand. The binder cut the crop and tied it in intae shaives. They were bigget intae stooks, ten tae a stook for corn and barley, twelve for wheat. The stooks were bigget so's the sun at aboot een o'clock shone doon the middle. This wis so's baith sides wid get the sun and dry aff. Fan they were dry the shaives were cairted tae the stackyaird in coup cairts wi their harvest frames fitted, or on ony flat larry tae. The stacks were bigget a fit or mair aff the grund on *stachles* wi a widden boss in the middle. The stachles were made o steen and looked like mushrooms wi a stalk and a roond tap. Fowk yaise them for gairden ornaments noo. Planks o wid were laid across the stachles and the shaives were bigget up wi the heids tae the inside and slopin tae the ootside tae shed ony watter that got inside and were theekit wi wheat strae tae throw aff the rain. They were feenished aff wi a knot at the tap in the shape o a wee cross or a thistle. The stacks settled doon eftir a while and if they werna properly bigget they wid nod tae ae side. They were tied doon wi criss-crossed strae raips, later '*sparty*' or esparto grass raips. They cud be yaised year eftir year but had tae be hung up somewye oot o the wye o rats and mice or the next year ye wid nae naething but bitties, nae yaise for onything. Ye did a sma threshin wi the barn mill a mornin or twa ilkae week tae get strae for beddin. The grain wis bagged and pit in the corn laft until there wis aneuch tae sell. The horse ging wisna yaised but sma paraffin engines drove the mills. Fan the traivelin mill cam roond ye needed 14 tae 16 fowk tae work it so ye had twa wifies lowsin shaives, and twa or three lads were borrowed fae the next ferm.

> There's horse mulls and watter mulls
> But the steam mull beats them a'
> It threshes the strae and bags the corn
> And bla's the caff awa

The grain wis pit intae big railway bags that had tae be cairried upstair intae the corn laft. Corn weyed 1½ hunderwecht, barley 2 hunderwecht and wheat 2¼ hunderwecht, a killer for onybody tae cairry, but especially a young loun or an aulder lad. It wis sheer slavery but daft buggers wid compete wi een anither tae show aff fat strong men they were, tae naebody's benefit but the fermers'. Twa lads got the bag on yere back wi the help o a stick or whiles there wis a contraption like a porter's barra wi a ratchet, ca'd an *orraman*. Afore balers were yaised the strae was bigget intae a lang *soo* tae be yaised for animal beddin.

At tattie hairst in October there were squads o wifies and schuil bairns tae dae the liftin, the horsemen worked the spinner digger and the cairts. The tatties no selt at the time were pitted until early the next year, happit wi layers o earth and wheat strae tae keep the frost oot. Tattie dressin wis daen aside the pits ootside of coorse, and cud be a damned cauld job if ye werna movin aboot diggin the tatties oot o the pit wi a *scuip*. That wis a graip wi roond ballies on the prongs so's nae tae damage the tatties. There were nae mechanical tattie dressin machines. The tatties were thrown on tae a *harp*. That wis a riddle that kept back the bigger tatties. They were bagged intae the tattie merchant's bags. Ony broken eens were picked oot and yaised for cattle feed. The big tatties gaed for ware, the medium eens for seed and the sma *chats* were back pitted tae be yaised for seed tae. The little boolies o tatties were yaised for pigs' meat or jist thrown awa.

Cattlers spent maist o their time inside fae late October tae early April. The cattle were fed inside in the byre and the coort for aboot seven month o the year. The dairy kye, breedin stock, and ony beasts for show were kept in the byre. The sta's had tae be muckit oot ilkae day and the muck pit in the midden. The store and feedin stirks and stots were kept louse in the coort. Fresh beddin wis pit doon ilkae day but the coort wis only cleared oot aboot October tae January and cairted oot tae dung the fields far ye were tae plant neeps and tatties. It wis a' duin wi the graip. If ye dug ower deep ye cud hardly lift the graip oot, hence the sayin *"come dung or brak graip"*. The cattle were fed oat strae, hey, neeps and cattle cake and some bruised barley, but they were maistly fattened on neeps. The neeps were hashed wi a manual neep hasher, there wis nae machinery until weel eftir the war. The cattler only got ae weekend aff in the month. He started at six in the mornin and had his breakfast aboot seven. He had an oor and a half at denner time, but in winter loused at half past fower. In summer fan the cattle were a' oot on grass he looked roond his parks in the mornin, sorted ony fences, and then reported tae the gaffer tae dae orra wark.

The end o the bothies

IT WAS MECHANISATION EFTIR THE WAR that brocht aboot the feenish o the bothy. There werna mony tractors afore the 1939–45 war. Wull Arnot at Fithie had a 1020 International mainly yaised for pu'in the grubber. The gaffer Geordie Leslie insisted on drivin it himsel, but drove it straicht through the dyke, grubber and a'. The wheels hadna tyres but metal *spuds* ye were supposed tae tak aff afore gaen on the public roads, that wis a fell palaver. Nether Careston jist afore the war had a rubber tyred Massey-Harris but durin the war they cudna replace the tyres. Newton o Boysack had a Case in 1943. John Mackie o the Bent had the first tractor-drawn combine jist afore the war. His wis the maist mechanised ferm in the haill country, no jist Scotland. Durin the war there werna muckle mair tractors, except far the government payed tae brack in new grund for cultivation. The factories were a' ower busy makin munitions. Eftir the war maist ferms had at least ae tractor yaised in heavy wark far ye needed three or fower horse tae pu the binder or the grubber. The foreman got the first tractor of coorse, but he micht find his kists thrown oot o the bothy, seein as he cudna claim tae be a horseman ony langer! Some ferms gaed ower completely tae tractors, overnicht ye micht say. Mackie o Benshie bocht fower new Fordson Majors, replacin a' the horse at eence in 1947. Guaranteed prices, tattie and milk marketin boards, gied the fermers a surer income than afore the war so the cheenge wis fairly rapid and gin 1950 there were few horse aroond.

THE TRACTOR

Last year I had a pair o' horse
The finest in the shire,
And we made a bonnie picture
At the harrows and the ploo,
I was never in a hurry,
And I whistled and I sang,
A' the lilts aboot the lassies,
Ah — but that's a' feenished noo.

Chorus
It's the tractor, the tractor,
And twenty miles an oor,
And the noise and the stink,
And the stoor — stoor — stoor.

I'd rather ha'e my bonnie pair,
And wear the corduroys,
A chap was proud tae haud the ploo,
And tak' things at his ease,
For you canna cock your bonnet
Sittin' in a tractor seat,
And your face just like a paddock,
Wi' the smoke and grime and grease.

Chorus

Tae start wi ye didna need mony less fowk because the tractors were haulin auld horse machinery and coup cairts adapted at the local smiddy and joiner's shop, but be the 1950s tractors near a' had power-drive and hydraulic lift and a haill new range o implements, multiple ploos and elevator tattie diggers, and syne self-propelled combines replaced the binders, so the horse becam a rare sicht and less fowk were needed on the ferms. It wisna until aboot the mid-1950s that tractors wi a front shovel were yaised tae muck oot the coorts and middens instead o men wi graips, and muck-spreaders did the work o six men on the fields. Mechanical elevators, tattie-dressin machines and neep hashers a' saved time and manpoo'er. But some places still kept horse. Friock Mains had twa tractors but still had a pair o horse up tae 1958 fan the horseman had a lang illness and they were selt. Spence at Commieston had horse up tae aroond 1960 but the lest place tae work wi naething but horse wis Carnegie o Arrat richt up tae 1964. Gin that time they were sic a rare sicht fowk cam fae far and wide tae see them, and newspaper lads tae photograph them, especially at hairst time. Arrat must hae been the lest sizable ferm in Scotland tae yaise naething but horse.

As the number o men needed on the ferms gaed doon, the bothies were duin awa wi. Single lads were gien a cottar hoose tae themsel, or atween twa o them. There were mair hooses, includin Cooncil hooses so fowk didna need tae pit aff gettin married for want o a hoose in the country, so there werna sae mony single lads tae accommodate. A few bothies were fully modernised for a single chap, some are still lived in the day, at

Hervieston Kineff for een. Arrat had the lest horse bothy, up tae 1964, but there were tractor bothies tae, but few and far atween eftir aboot 1960. Twa aulder unmerried lads bade in the bothy at Windyedge up tae aboot 1972 fan een got merried and the bothy wis abandoned. The lest wis maybe at Mains o Careston far an auld mannie bade up tae 1978. It had electric licht and inside watter but nae lavvy, jist the coort as in the auld days. Gin then, bothies were a thing o the past. Naebody cud ever regret the passin o the bothies, but some lads look back on their bothy days as happy days a' the same.

ITS LONELY AT NICHT IN THE BOTHY

Oh fan I gaed hame tae Ardo
Well the boss had nae a clue
He cudna back a tractor, cairt,
There's nae wye he cud ploo.
Therefore I got a' the work tae dae
That suited me jist fine
An' I bade in a little timmer bothy.

Chorus
> *For the cauld winds they bla in aneth*
> *My timmer bothy door.*
> *An' the moosies they djeuk in an' oot*
> *The knotholes in the fluir.*
> *But that's no the warst o' bein here*
> *Discomforts I can thole,*
> *For its lonely at nicht in the bothy.*

Noo I sort the mannie's fancy bulls
I put them oot for Perth.
I ken that I'm the best show man
That ever walked the earth.
But fan a' the judgin's ower
An' a' the silver's won,
It's back tae my little timmer bothy.

Chorus

61

Noo I've nae wife tae tie me doon
So I'm aye on the loose,
An' nearly every nicht I'm doon
At Waldie's public hoose.
But ye canna blame a man
For takin comfort far he can,
For its lonely at nicht in the bothy.

Chorus

Charlie Allan

(Although written about Ardo in Buchan rather than the Ardo near Brechin, and there were no timber bothies in this district, the words of the above song reflect the situation of the last solitary bothy dwellers in the 1970s.)

PART 3
Appendices

The Horseman's Word

THIS WAS THE PLOUGHMEN'S SECRET SOCIETY, to which at one time the majority of horsemen once belonged. But many of the secrets of initiation were given away in 1908 by a former Aberdeenshire ploughman living in London. A Horseman was supposed to have absolute mastery over horses but some were more skilled than others. However, the secrets of how to master horses is still a mystery to the non-initiated. Several notes and articles have been published on the subject. Even so, some of my informants did not think I should publish a section on the Horseman's Word in case anyone thought that they had divulged any secrets and they might be *"thrappled wi a couplin tow"*. One had been *'made'* a freemason, a horseman and a curler and took them in that order of secrecy and seriousness. The Horseman's Word existed all over the arable areas of eastern Scotland from Orkney to Berwickshire and had an English equivalent, but was not organised on anything but a local basis. Some writers seem to think it was peculiar to, or lasted longer in the north-east. To dispel this bias I must point out that a young Angus ploughman was *'made'* a Horseman in Fife in the late 1950s, and over half my informants, when asked, admitted to having been initiated as Horsemen. Others denied any knowledge of the Horseman's Word, although most had been horsemen in the general sense, some may have been evasive. The Horseman's Word seems to have continued as long as there were horses around but can only have started in the district from around 1770 when horses began to replace oxen as draught animals, a process which was virtually complete in the district by around 1800, but in the north-east not until the 1840s or even later.

The details seem to have differed from district to district but the basics were similar. A minimum of three Horsemen were needed to initiate new members. The newcomer had to bring a loaf of bread, a bottle of whisky and sometimes a candle. He would have been asked once he got his first pair and aged from 16 to 45. He was sat blindfolded, sometimes on an upturned bushel measure. He was asked several questions and if he answered correctly was administered the oath. He had to swear not to divulge any secrets given to him or ever write them down, nor to see the Word given to anyone except those who worked with horses including vets, farriers and cavalrymen, and to keep it a secret from all his relations, male and female. He was never to abuse horses or see anyone else doing so without saying anything. He was to attend meetings at three days notice. If he broke the promise his flesh was to be torn apart by wild horses, his heart cut through with a horseman's knife, and his bones to be buried within the flow of the tide. He finally got to "*shak hands wi auld Horny*" (the Devil), a piece of wood covered with animal skin or the foot of a calf or a goat. He could then be given the '*word*' which could stop a horse in its tracks or quieten a runaway, sometimes "*both in one*", signifying the unity of horse and man. Afterwards everyone had a drink to finish off the occasion.

The initiation was often carried out around Martinmas (28th November), and usually in a barn, "*through the caff hoose door*" as the song '*Nicky Tams*' says. But in the late 1920s in Angus, at least one man was initiated in a room in a hotel. The ceremony was also supposed to take place on a Sunday, or at least between sunset on Saturday and sunrise on Monday. An odd number of persons, preferably thirteen, had to be present. In some districts the initiates pawed and whinnied like horses, at the door. There were secret signs and expressions by which another brother could be identified, just as the freemasons have, one was called the *foal's lick*. The most detailed account of the Horseman's Word is by Hamish Henderson the folklorist and he stresses the anti-Christian and diabolic elements in the words spoken, but in recent times this may not have been taken too literally. At one time potions and powders were given to horses to make them appear unwell or disabled, as a way of getting back at the farmer. Generally speaking the Word was simply another expression of the pride the horsemen took in their ability to work horses, which bound them together against outsiders.

Bothy Ballads

ABOUT EIGHTY-FIVE PERCENT of so-called bothy ballads which recount life on particular named farms, can be located between the Dee and the Spey, where there were very few bothies, and only a handful come from the real bothy areas. So the term *bothy ballad* is a misnomer, Gavin Greig preferred to call them ploughmen's songs and they are otherwise known as cornkisters. John Ord collected many songs from the north-east, the Mearns, Angus and Perthshire and entitled his collection 'Bothy Ballads'. They may all have been sung in bothies but few are specific to any area or relate to bothy or farm life. Peter Hall has suggested that the reason so many songs such as *'Drumdelgie'* (which pillory a particular farmer) were created, was because of the prevalence of six-monthly feeing and that the songs were sung as a warning. This may well have been true, but since six-monthly feeing was also the norm for single men farther south, why are there comparatively few bothy ballads from other areas? Could it be that there were fewer interested collectors working in these areas? No doubt many songs could have been lost and forgotten before anyone ever wrote them down and they died with the bothy system. However the reason that there were so many collectors from within and outwith the north-east who collected songs there was probably that it just had a stronger song-singing and song-making tradition than any other area for some unaccountable local cultural reason. William J. Milne had heard songs sung in Angus farm kitchens in the 1840s but he said he had never heard a greater number of Scotland's fine old songs than in the Formartine farm kitchen where he was feed in 1851. If people could memorise many old songs it is likely that they could make up or adapt songs to recall their own experiences.

Many types of song were popular in the bothies of Angus and the Mearns, and other areas to the south, but songs such as the '*Dying Ploughboy*' and the many commemorating ploo'men laddies and their lasses were always very popular, as were north-east cornkisters like '*The Muckin o Geordies Byre*' and '*Nicky Tams*' even if Wull Tams was the local expression. There are however a few work-related bothy ballads which were composed locally and mention particular farms in the district, the horses and people on them. Some were collected in the north-east and had got corrupted on the way such as '*Mararfray*' which was obviously Morphie, which stands on a hill in the Mearns, not far from Montrose. There is also a plagiarised version of '*Mormond Braes*' — 'Clova's Braes'. But there are a few other local bothy ballads in the strict definition: '*The Banks o the Esk*' (Glen Coull is no longer a distillery but a grain mill); '*The Mill o Lour*', is said to have been very popular in Angus and Perthshire, and variations were adapted to other farms there; '*Barry Mill*' is a fragment of another work-related song collected by Colin Gibson. There may be others which are in someone's memory and have never been written down.

Other bothy ballads were about courting: '*Between Stanhyve and Laurencekirk*' is less specific as to place but warns of the jealousy of the 'maiden', the farmer's unmarried daughter; '*Riccarton Woods*' are on the *Slug* road between Stonehaven and Banchory; '*The Bonny Woods o Hatton*' which mention Cadem (Caldhame) and Leather (Luther) make it plain it was the Hatton in Marykirk or Aberluthnott parish in the Howe o the Mearns; '*The Bothy Lads o Forfar*' is another type of song which seems to record an otherwise unknown case where men were transported to Botany Bay for stealing tatties! Forfar refers to the county rather than the town. This may be the earliest of the ballads included here, which mostly date from the 1830s to the 1880s. The verse which prefaces the chapter on '*Bothy lads and ither fowk aboot the place*' is in the tradition of work-related bothy ballads but was not sung and does not scan, it was composed in the bothy at Reidhall farm, Stracathro in

1921–22 by men who sang and apparently made up songs. '*The Banks of the Esk*' which was composed by the men on Murthill farm as late as around 1938, is very much in the old tradition of work-related bothy ballads. Some verse composed around 1900 and later is mere doggerel, not worth repeating. Several books of verse by ploughmen were published around 1890–1900 but none of the verse have the pithyness or down to earth Scots of the ballads included here, only a few refer to farm life or bothies, the best by John Kerr, a Laurencekirk bookseller and former bothy chiel it would seem. His verse is full of interesting and useful references to agricultural methods and life, but are extremely long so examples are not given here. With the exception of '*The Banks of the Esk*' it seems the ballad-making was very weak after 1900.

*MARAFRAY

THERE is a toon oot fae Montrose
It stands upon a brae
And the name that it gangs under
They ca' it Marafray.

> *Sing aeri-iritie adie man*
> *Sing iriti andi kay.*

The foremost pair aboot oor toon
They sweer they are the best
But gin they had the roons to gang
They'd be as bad's the rest man.

The seed time is comin' on
When we maun look alive
But they thought they wid get Jip to gang in the machine
But they got an awfu surprise man.

We hae a grieve aboot oor toon
They sweer he is the best
For to plan the wark to tarnish men
But the paintin' goes up his back, man.

Bell Lowe she rises in the mornin
Wi' a nose sae neat and fine
She jabbers and curses, habbers and sweers
Like a donkey gaun wrang in his mind, man.

The term time is comin' on
When we will get the brass
And we'll gang doon to Jean Lowe's
We'll hae a partin' glass man.

We'll hae a pairtin glass my lads
Likewise a jovial spree
And we'll bid farewell to the dairymaids
We left at *Marafree man.

*Morphie

CLOVA'S BRAES

As I gaed doon tae Farfar toon,
I heard a fair maid mournin',
And she was makin' sair complaint,
For her true love ne'er returnin'.
It's Clova's Braes where heather grows,
Where aft times I've been cheery,
It's Clova's Braes where heather grows,
And it's there I've lost my dearie.

> *Sae fare ye weel ye Clova's Braes*
> *Where aftimes I've been cheery,*
> *Fare ye weel, ye Clova's Braes*
> *For it's there I've lost my dearie.*

Oh, I'll put on my goon o' green,
It's a forsaken token,
And that will let the young men know
That the bands of love are broken.
There's mony a horse has snappert and fa'en,
And risen and gane fu' rarely,
There's mony a lass has lost her lad,
And gotten anither richt early.

68

There's as guid fish into the sea,
As ever yet was taken,
I'll cast my line and try again
I'm only ance forsaken.
Sae I'll gae doon tae Farfar Toon,
Where I was bred and born,
And there I'll get anither sweetheart
Will mairry me the morn!

ON THE BANKS O' THE ESK

ON the banks o' the Esk, near Glen Coull Distil,
There lives an auld mannie, and his name it is Wull,
A lauchn' auld mannie, aboot three score and ten,
But ye have tae be fee'd wi' him, afore him ye ken.

He's a great dairy farmer, he keeps thirty kye,
He farms Murthall Mains, and New Dyke forbye,
Murthall's no' a bad place, it's a place o' sharp land,
But Wullie's mair interested in gravel and sand.

He keeps three pair o' horses, and ane for the loon,
But like Wullie himsel' they were born far ower soon,
And mind it's nae joke for the boys on the Mains,
For they're sent to ca' gravel ilka day for it rains.

He's got a big sonsy dauchter, the flower o' the glen,
Likewise a bit maidie ca'd Lizzie McLean,
And the lads o' the bothy ne'er weary ava,
For the rats play teet bo' through the holes in the wa'.

But the term time will soon wear roond, and we will
        a win awa',
Frae auld Wullie, and his weety weather,
And gravel and sand an' a'.

69

THE MILL O' LOUR

WE a' agreed at Martinmas,
At Mill o' Lour to dwell,
They said it was a very fine place
But it turned out not so well.

> *Ah riddel doo, ill-dum, da-dee,*
> *Ah riddel doo, ill-dum, da-day.*

The Lour mill's a heavy mill,
And unco ill to ca';
Tho' we yoke a' the horses in
She'll hardly draw ava.

Sandy works the foremost pair,
They are a pair o' blues;
Altho' ye had them at your *wale
Ye wadna ken which to choose.

Jamie works the second pair,
A black ane and a broon;
There's no a cannier, trustier pair
In a' the country roun'.

Jess comes in ahint the lave,
She's ca'd the orra mare;
In winter when we're sheuchin' neeps
She rins like ony hare.

*choice, pick

BARRY MILL

Rize up i' the mornin'
A little efter three,
We up an' corn oor horses
An' back for a mug o' tea.

And when we ging tae Barry Mill,
We never pit aff time,
We reel them on and sweel them on,
An' back again gin nine.

BETWEEN STANEHIVE AND LAURENCEKIRK

BETWEEN Stanehive and Laurencekirk
Last term I did fee,
'Twas wi' a wealthy farmer,
His foreman for to be.
To work his twa best horses
Was what I had to do,
A task that I could manage weel
Both in the cart and ploo.

I worked my horses carefully,
And did my master please,
Excepting to some rants o' fun
That did his temper tease;
Until the month o' January,
As you may weel believe,
For courtin' wi' the servin' girl
We both did get our leave.

One night into the stable,
By tryst I met her there,
On purpose for to have some fun,
And guid advice to gie 'er;
Our master hearing o' the same,
To the stable he cam' o'er;
And he did give us both our leave
Out o' the stable door.

But it's not upon my master
That I lay all the blame,
It is the *maiden o' the place,
That high respected dame.
Since no sweetheart to her did come,
It grieved her sore to see
The happy moments that were spent
Between my love and me.

Come, all ye jolly ploughboys
That want to mend the fau't;
Be sure it is the maiden first
That ye maun court and daut;
For if ye court the servant first,
and gang the *maiden by,
Ye may be sure the term for you
Is quickly drawin' nigh.

Surely the times are gettin' hard
When courtin's ca'ed a crime;
For it has been practised noo
Guid ken's for hoo lang time;
But yon big toon abuin the road,
It is forbidden there;
And for feein' wi' yon farmer
I bid you a' beware.

*farmer's daughter

THE WOODS OF RICKARTON

COME, all ye jolly ploughman lads,
And listen to my rhyme;
The praises of your bonnie glen
I would be fain to sing.

For I dearly lo'e the heather hills,
And lasses leal and true,
That lo'e the bonnie laddie
That ca's the cairt and plough.

The bonnie woods o' Rickarton
I love to wander through,
To hear the blackbird whistle,
And the cushie curdle-doo.

To see the burnie winding clear,
The cowslips spring so sweet;
And to see the bonnie lassie
That I've trysted there to meet.

We ploughman lads are hardy chiels,
We're clean as well as clad;
We like to please our masters,
And see our horses fed.

But we dearly lo'e the girlies,
And meet them on the sly,
And get a kindly crack wi' them
At the milking o' the kye.

For ilka Jockie has a Jean,
A Bawbie or a Nell;
I hae a lass I dearly lo'e,
Though her name I winna tell.

But it winna be yon dandy lass
That'll wile my heart awa',
She's foul and clorty at her wark,
Though Sunday she gangs braw.

She wadna marry a ploughman lad,
'Cause she has a puckle gear;
But if it wasna for her father's cash
There's few wad gang to see her.

But she need not be so mighty prood,
And cast her head so high,
For there's no ae lad in a' the glen
But would gae pass her by.

But she'll maybe get some farmer's son
Mair suiting to her mind;
And I hope she'll soon get married
If she so feel inclined.

But he's very welcome to her,
And her muckle †tocher too;
He's free to wear out my auld shoon
Since I hae gotten new.

Now the harvest it is over,
And winter's coming on,
The lang dark nichts will soon be here,
And I'll get wanton fun.

Among the lasses in the glen,
They're all so trig and neat;
But we winna cross the Cowie
For fear our feet get weet.

Success to the farmer,
And much prosperity;
And health unto the ploughboy
That works for meat and fee.

I wish the lassie happiness,
May she ne'er hae to rue,
That marries the bonnie laddie
That gangs whistling at the ploo.

†dowry

THE BONNIE WOODS O' HATTON

YE comrades and companions, and all ye females dear,
To my sad lamentations I pray ye give an ear;
Once I lo'ed a bonnie lass, I lo'ed her as my life,
It was my whole intentions to make her my wedded wife.

74

I courted wi' this bonnie lass a twelve months and a day,
Sometimes amang the green grass, sometimes amang
    the hay;
I courted her a lea-lang nicht and part o' the next day
Till she said, "My dearest Sandy, it's time you were
    away."

Says I, "My pretty Betsy, when will you set a time
When you and I'll get married, love, and hands together
    join;
You'll sit in our wee cottage and you'll neither spin nor
    sew,
While your ain kind-hearted hireman lad gangs whistling
    at the ploo."

There's Castem and there's Cadem Mills and Leather
    Mills likewise,
There are woods and waters mony more that's present to
    my eyes;
But the bonnie woods o' Hatton, they a' grow green in
    May,
'Twas there the bonnie lassie lived that stole my heart
    away.

I'll speak about yon bonnie lass though I be far awa,
I'll speak about yon bonnie lass to those she never saw,
I'll tell them that I lo'ed her well although she proved
    untrue,
And left me doon by Hatton's woods my follies for to rue.

But blessings on yon bonnie lass, wherever she may be,
I wish no evil unto her although she slighted me;
I only hope she'll say some day, before that she does dee,
"I wish I'd wed yon hireman lad that sang sae sweet
    to me."

THE BOTHY LADS O' FORFAR

IT'S ten pair upon our place,
And ten strong able men;
It takes five o' us to light a fire,
And five o' us to *scran.

> *O Earm, O Dearm,*
> *Fal the diddle Earm,*
> *O Earm, O Dearm,*
> *Fal the diddle ee.*

Ae nicht we were in the tattie hoose,
Our creels were nearly fu',
When Tattie Jock cries oot, —
"Hi' lads, you're nearly fu'".

It's ten policemen being sent for,
But only nine did come;
There werena fit to turn us about,
We were so able men.

It's Jocky being among us,
The blithest one I saw,
He had to leave his country,
'Cause he couldna stand the law.

It's now our summons' come,
And now our sentence' passed;
It's sixteen years' hard labour.
It's all the time at last.

As we sat in the top o' the coach,
I heard the coachboy say,
'Twas a pity to see such able men
Rolled down to Botany Bay.

*scrounge

But when we arrive at Botany Bay,
We'll send some letters home,
And tell our parents all our hardships
Since we left our native home.

The Angus and Mearns dialect

THERE IS NO RECOGNISED NAME for this dialect but it is the southernmost form of Northern Scots but quite distinct from North-east Scots which is spoken over a larger area and is more readily recognised outside its home area. The dialect is spoken over most of Angus, except for the south-western fringes bordering on Perthshire, and in the southern part of the Mearns. Speakers of North-east Scots, even in Stonehaven, which is just beyond the dialect boundary, have been known to accuse speakers of this dialect of being 'Fifers' as it sounds to them like Midland Scots. Conversely, in southern Scotland the dialect can sometimes be mistaken for 'Aberdonian' or North-east Scots. It is impossible to convey on paper the exact sound or intonation of the dialect. It lacks, however, the curious intonation of North-east Scots but is also different to the Mid Scots dialect spoken in Perthshire. It contains many good old Scots sounds such as the *ch* in licht, bricht, hicht, falling out of use among younger folk.

One general characteristic is the replacement of wh by f only in question words: fa=who, fan=when, foo=why, far=where, fat/fit=what, and fatten/fitten or fatna=which but not in other words. So *whitteret* (weasel), white and whisky rather than North-east *futret, fite* and *fisky. Fat* for what is the general tendency in Angus, especially in the Forfar area, otherwise it is a flatter vowel than the sharper *fit* of North-east Scots. One usage the dialect has in common with North-east Scots is the short flat a as in ca, wa, ba, rather than Mid Scots caw, waw, baw, for English call, wall, ball. Another is canna, dinna, winna for can't, don't, won't rather than Mid Scots canny, dinny, winny found in Perthshire and further south.

The dialect has a wider range of vowel sounds than any other Scots dialect. It can be distinguished from dialects to the north and south by the use of the diphthong I have spelt *ui*, which is like the vowel in the French *peu* and German *schön*. It is used in place of English *oo*, which in Mid Scots becomes *i* and in North-east Scots *ee*. So we have muin, shuin, spuin, schuil and ruif, a longer vowel than in Mid Scots and very different from the North-east Scots meen, sheen, speen, skweel and reef. This vowel sound was once also found in *tui, dui, yuised* but Mid Scots *tae, dae, yaised* have replaced it. In Montrose and the coastal villages of Ferryden, Johnshaven, Gourdon, Bervie and Catterline these become *toe, doe, yosed*, while buits become *boets*, but this peculiarity is not found to landward, even in the same parishes. Early this century older folk still pronounced the *k* in knee, knife but this was pronounced more like *t* but with the tongue on the roof of the mouth. A few older folk still call a clock, especially a steeple clock, a *knock* but about the only time the k before n is still heard is in the expression "*yere fair knackin on*" meaning you're really rushing about.

The vocabulary, where it differs from other Scots dialects has some words in common with North-east Scots but can often be very different, and in some cases the same word means something entirely different: *staig* meant a young horse of either sex not broken into harness and the *staigger* was the man who trained or broke in staigs, but in the north-east *staig* meant a breeding stallion and the *staigger* was the man who accompanied it around farms. *Bannock* is the usual word for a hard-baked thin oatcake, while to the north and south it means a soft cake or scone of wheat or barley flour; *breid* means baker-made wheat loaves, sometimes called loaf-breid but in the north east *breid* means oatcakes and wheat bread is *loaf*; *theevil* is the wooden stick for stirring porridge, but in the north-east this is a *spurtle*, which by contrast was an iron implement for toasting bannocks in the district in question. Often there are two words in common use, the first quoted is apparently the original local word, the second the north-east word: peesie or teuchat (peewit), shillie or chaffie (chaffinch), hornie-golach or forkie-taillie (earwig), creeshie-meallie or skirlie (oatmeal fried with onions), titlin or sharger (smallest of a litter). Many other words are peculiar to the district or only parts of it such as *nettercap* or *netterie* for spider.

Within the district straddling the two counties there are few differences in vocabulary, mainly in intonation and pronounciation. Folk just on the north side of the North Water have a slightly more '*north*' intonation than their Angus neighbours, although this is more perceptible in some individuals than in others. Mearns folk find the dialect around Forfar discernibly more distinct from their own than that of north Angus, but the same is true within Angus. North-east Scots has penetrated from north of the Mounth, where it developed in isolation, into the southern Mearns only in the last hundred years or so and has strongly influenced the local dialect even in the Howe o the Mearns. A steady southwards movement of farm workers from the north-east, mainly from about the 1880s to the 1960s, caused this dialect change. The most obvious shibboleth is the use of *quine*, standard from Auchenblae and Fordoun northwards, rather than *lassie* used to the south. The few natives of Catterline on the coast speak the Mearns tongue like the Gourdon folk to the south, but five miles to the north in Stonehaven North-east Scots is spoken. Inland from Catterline at Roadside of Kinneff, youngsters admit to the use of *quine* or *lassie* and have a quite strong '*north*' intonation. On the farms north of the Bervie Water, and many to the south, it is difficult to find a farmworker who is *not* a native of Aberdeenshire. So many children have parents who are both from Aberdeenshire that they too speak North-east Scots, even in Angus this is true of a few families. In the area inland of Stonehaven there is, however, a mixture of Mearns and North-east vocabulary with a strong '*north*' intonation. The terms *yoke* and *louse*, originally used by horsemen to mean the start and finish of a period of work have passed into common parlance applying to the working day, even among townsfolk in the district. A verb *bothyin* has developed from the noun bothy. It is used by men to describe their efforts at cooking and housekeeping when their wife is away from home: *"I'm jist bothyin the noo, so dinna mind the state o the hoose"*.

A note on spelling in Part 2

Hardly any prose has ever been written in the dialect so a recognised spelling has never been developed. In particular there are several vowel sounds not easy to convey. The *ui* diphthong in *spuin, muin* etc. is explained above. The *ng* on the end of words is not pronounced so the g has not been written. The Old Scots equivalent was *-and* or *-end* and so it is really a *d* that has been dropped from older speech. Likewise the hard g after n in the middle of a word is never pronounced, so the *ng* in the word single is pronounced as in singer.

Standard English spelling has been retained for some words but they are pronounced differently, thus: *wash* rhymes with English crash or bash and is not pronounced *wawsh*; war becomes *waar* not *wawr*; *fire* and *tyre* become *fiyir* and *tyir*; *mower* rhymes with *tower* and *warm* sounds like *warum*; push and pull rhyme with hush and hull; the vowel in *rise* is like that in nice but longer; milk and mill sound more like mulk and mull, although the usual English spelling has been used.

Inverted commas to indicate a letter missing from the English spelling has been used as little as possible and only for the sake of clarity as in *pu'ed* for pulled and in *a'* meaning all to distinguish it from the definite article, but *o* for of. The word *in* has been spelt consistently but the *n* is often not pronounced, as before *the*. The word *and* has also been so spelt although the *d* is sometimes dropped. The vowel in the words hey (hay) and pey (pay) has no real English equivalent but is like the i in bite or hight, but longer. The vowel in words such as *wye* rhymes with pie. In Scots the letter *l* after a vowel or *ll* at the end of a word becomes an extension of the vowel so *folk, stall, bolster*, even if spelt that way should be pronounced *fowk, sta, bowster*, but have been spelt the latter way to make the dialect pronounciation absolutely clear. Note that *acre, stair* and *horse* are all plural as well as singular, just as English *fish* and *sheep* are. Note also that porridge is always a plural noun, so is referred to as *them*, not *it*. With the help of the glossary it should be possible for anyone to follow the text of Part 2 of this book.

Glossary

abody	everybody
achday	everyday
affa	awful, very
afore	before
ahent	behind
ain	own
aise	ashes (pronounced *ace*)
aisier	easier
alow	below
amuin	amongst
aneuch	enough
arles	token payment of engagement to work
athing	everything
athoot	without
ava	at all
bade	stayed, remained, resided
bagwallopers	potato harrows, so called from the way they forced a ploughman to walk down a central drill
bannocks	oatcakes
barkit	having a skin, or skinned
besom	floor brush
bide	stay, remain, reside
bigg	build
bigget	built
blind-drift	snowstorm impossible to see through
bobbies	policemen
bocht	bought
bosses	triangular wooden frames on which stacks were built
bowster	bolster

bra	grand
brander	grating, grille
brecham	horse collar
breeks	trousers
breer	sprout
brocht	brought
brose	oatmeal mixed with boiling water, salt etc.
brui	brew, liquid in cooking
brui	broom
ca	drive
ca'd	called
calders	cold porridge
cam	came
cauld steer	oatmeal mixed with cold water
chield	chap, fellow
chaip	cheap
chopin	about 1½ Imperial pints
claes	clothes
claeser	clothes chest
clootie dumplin	large treacle dumpling boiled in a cloth (cloot)
cole	loose pile of hay built around a wooden frame
cookie	small bun
coorse	coarse
corn	oats, grain
coup	tip-up, fall
crack	chat, talk
creesh	fat, grease
creeshie-meallie	oatmeal and onions fried in fat
cud	could
daidlin	rough treatment
dame	girl friend
darg	task, duty
dicht	wipe
djeuks	ducks
doo	pigeon, dove
doon	down
doup	backside
dreel	drill
duin	done, worn out
eftir	after
et	ate

fae	from
faird	afraid
fan	when
far	where
fat	what
fee	engagement to work
feed	engaged to work
fell	quite, rather
find	feel
firlot	quarter boll (about 25 lbs weight for oatmeal)
fit 1	what
fit 2	foot
flair	floor
foo	why, how
frenchies	condoms
gaed	went
galluses	braces
garred	made to, caused to
gied	gave
gin	by the time that (hard *g*)
ging	go
grat	cried
grubber	cultivator
guid	good
hae	have
haen	had
hag	brushwood
haffie	half loaf, plain bread loaf
haims	metal part of horse collar
haip	heap
hairst	harvest
hake	hay rack
hale	whole
hale-watter	whole water (very heavy rain)
hame	home
hanle	handle
hap	cover
hash 1	cut up
hash 2	overwork
hing	hang
hoo	how

ingan	onion
Irishman's rise	a drop in wages
jug	mug
kent	knew
kick	agreed monthly advance from six months wages
kist	chest
kye	cows
lat	let
lathie	laddie, boy (obsolete pronounciation)
lauch	laugh
ley	lea, fallow
lib	castrate
licht 1	light
licht 2	alight, land
loup	jump
louse	to loosen harness from horse, finish work (louze)
mair	more
maisered	measured
maist	most
mavie	thrush
mealer	meal chest
meat	food
melodian	button-key squeeze-box
midser	midyokin snack
midyokin	break or snack in the middle of a yoke
moothie	mouth organ
muckle	much, big, many
nae	not
neeps	turnips
oaffie	dry privy
oors 1	ours
oors 2	hours
oot	out
or	until
orra	ordinary, spare, odd
orrabaist	an old horse used for odd jobs
orrabaister	person who drove the orrabaist
orrals	left overs
orraman	general farm labourer
orrawark	general farm work
ower	over, too

pannie	firewood (panwood), week about on bothy chores
park	field
peesie	peewit
pictairnie	black-headed gull
plaised	pleased
poke	bag, sack
press	cupboard
puffie-tooties	fancy cakes
raised	angry
ranns	cod roe
redd	tidy up
reek	smoke
rinds	reins
roch	rough
sair	sore
saftie	soft white roll
sark	shirt
scadded	scalded, burned, rubbed sore
seek	sick
semmit	vest
shairn	cow dung
shewin	sewing
sholt	pony
sic	such
sixer	six monthly term
skirlie	oatmeal and onions fried in fat
skitters	diarrhoea
sma'er	smaller
sna'in	snowing
soo	sow (long pile of straw)
sort	set in order, repair
sowens	gruel made from fermented flour off oat husks
sta	stall, as in a stable
staig	young horse, not broken in
staigger	man who trained staigs
steepies	bread soaked in hot milk
stirk	young cattle beast, kept for fattening
stot	young bullock
stovies	potatoes stewed with fat and onions
sud	should
swey	fireplace crane to hang pots from

syne	then
tatties	potatoes
teuchat	peewit
term	six months engagement to work
thaits	traces
thaiter	trace-horse
theek	thatch
thole	suffer, bear with
thir	these
thrappled	throttled
till	to
tow	string, cord
trait	treat
trump	jews harp
wattery	(noun) W.C.
whiles	sometimes, occasionally
wid 1	wood
wid 2	would
widna	wouldn't
wifie	woman
win	gain, get
wis 1	wish
wis 2	was (wiz)
wisna	wasn't
wull tams	leather straps belted below the knee to support the weight of trousers
yaise	use
yaisyil	usual
yirned milk	curds and whey
yoke	to put harness on horses, start work
yokin	spell of work with horses, of 4 to 5 hours

Placenames

Aiberdeen	Aberdeen
Aigle	Edzell
Bowshin	Bolshan
Benshie	Ballinshoe
Farfar	Forfar
Fetterie	Fettercairn
Friock	Friockheim

Kirrie	Kirriemuir
Lowrnie	Laurencekirk
Skite	Drumlithie
Steenhyve	Stonehaven

Sources and Background Reading

PART 1

Monographs and reports etc.

A. C. Cameron — *The history of Fettercairn.* Paisley: J. & R. Farlane, 1899

David Kerr Cameron — *The ballad and the plough.* London: V. Gollancz, 1978   — *The cornkister days.* London: V. Gollancz, 1984

Ian Carter — *Farm life in North East Scotland 1840–1914.* Edinburgh: John Donald, 1979

T. M. Devine (ed.) — *Farm servants and labour in Lowland Scotland 1770–1914.* Edinburgh: John Donald, 1984

John Duncan — *The Scottish peasantry their joys and hardships, told by sons of the soil. in* Contributions to the press, Forfar Public Library. (Press cuttings, 1886–)

A. Fenton & B. Walker — *The rural architecture of Scotland.* Edinburgh: John Donald, 1981

W. R. Fraser — *History of the parish and burgh of Laurencekirk.* Edinburgh: Blackwood, 1880

James Headrick — *A general view of the agriculture of the county of Angus or Forfarshire.* Edinburgh, 1813

James Inglis — *Oor ain folk.* Edinburgh: D. Douglas, 1894

G. H. Kinnear — *Kincardineshire.* (Cambridge County Geographies) Cambridge: U.P., 1921

William J. Milne — *Reminiscences of an old boy: being autobiographical stories of Scots rural life 1832–1856.* Forfar, 1901

C. A. Mollyson — *The parish of Fordoun . . .* Aberdeen: J. P. Smith, 1893

J. Robb — *The cottage the bothy and the kitchen.* Edinburgh: Blackwood, 1861

George Robertson — *A general view of the agriculture of Kincardineshire or the Mearns.* London, 1813

R. S. Skirving — *Essay VII Report on the present state of the agriculture of Scotland.* Highland and Agricultural Society, 1878

Harry Stuart — *Agricultural labourers as they were, are and ought to be in their social condition.* Talk given to the Forfarshire Agricultural Association. June, 1853

Alan Tragham — *Farm labourers' bothies in Strathmore, Angus and the Carse of Gowrie, Perthshire.* Thesis presented for B.A.Hons. Architecture, University of Dundee, 1979

Statistical Accounts and Census records

Statistical Account of Scotland: Angus 1790–94; Kincardineshire 1790–94

New Statistical Account of Scotland: Forfarshire & Kincardineshire 1835–44

Third Statistical Account of Scotland: The County of Kincardine 1950–55

Third Statistical Account of Scotland: The County of Angus 1960–65

Census of Scotland 1841, 1861, 1871, 1881 selected parishes Angus and Mearns

PART 2

Monographs and reports

Jessie Buchanan — (*Memories of farm workers lives, mainly at Broomhill, near Montrose*) Typescript report, 1965 Country Life Archive, Royal Museum of Scotland

A. Smith — *Forty years in Kincardineshire 1911–1951: a bothy loon's life story.* Collieston: Caledonian Books, 1990

Information from:

Andra Archer
Andra Beattie
Bob Brandie
Stan Brown
Harry Bushnell
Bob Carnegie
Andy Church
Eck Henry
Wull Foreman
Bob MacDonald
Bob Mathers
Sandy Murray
Wull Nicoll
John Ogilvie
Frank Ritchie
Sam Robertson
Frank Ross
Jim Smart
Wull Spalding
Wull Stark
Ed Thomson
Geordie Watson
Sy Welsh

PART 3

The Horseman's Word

A. Fenton — *The Horseman's Word* in *Discovering Scotland*, 36 1990 p. 936

H. Henderson — *The ballad and the folk: the oral tradition* in E. J. Cowan — *The people's past*. Edinburgh: Polygon, 1980

Bothy ballads

Books of verse:

Robert W. Blaikie — *Lea-rig fancies: the rhymes of a farm servant.* Brechin: D. H. Edwards, 1990

James & William Clark — *Leisure musings by two ploughmen . . . natives of Fordoun. 2nd Ed.* Montrose: Standard Press, 1894

John Kerr — *Reminiscences of a wanderer . . . Part Three.* Aberdeen: J. Avery, 1892

Collections and comments on ballads:

Peter A. Hall — *Folk song of the North east farm servants in the 19th century,* Thesis presented for M.Litt. University of Aberdeen, 1985

George B. Lowe — *The bothy songs and ballads of Angus* in The Angus Christmas Annual, 1979. Arbroath: Herald Press, 1979

Emily B. Lyle & Peter A. Hall (eds.) — *The Greig-Duncan folk song collection Vol. 3.* Aberdeen: A.U.P., 1987

John Ord — *The bothy songs and ballads . . .* Paisley: Gardner, 1930

The Angus and Mearns dialect

Personal observation of local speech and pronounciation

The Concise Scots Dictionary. Aberdeen: A.U.P., 1985